AUDIO ACCESS INCLUDED

FIRST 50 SCALES

YOU SHOULD PLAY ON GUITAR

One-of-a-kind collection of accessible, must-know scale shapes used to play licks and solos in countless rock, pop, blues, folk, and jazz songs

by Doug Boduch

To access audio, visit:
www.halleonard.com/mylibrary

Enter Code
6777-0956-9878-9222

ISBN 979-8-3501-0799-9

A Muse Group Company

Visit Hal Leonard Online at
www.halleonard.com

World headquarters, contact:
Hal Leonard
7777 West Bluemound Road
Milwaukee, WI 53213
Email: info@halleonard.com

In Europe, contact:
Hal Leonard Europe Limited
Dettingen Way
Bury St Edmunds, Suffolk, IP33 3YB
Email: info@halleonardeurope.com

In Australia, contact:
Hal Leonard Australia Pty. Ltd.
4 Lentara Court
Cheltenham, Victoria, 3192 Australia
Email: info@halleonard.com.au

CONTENTS

INTRODUCTION

Welcome to *First 50 Scales You Should Play on Guitar*. So, what exactly is a scale, and why is it important to include them in our guitar studies? Simply put, a scale is an ordered sequence of notes. When you sing "do, re, mi, fa, so, la, ti, do," that's a scale. (It's a major scale to be specific, but we'll learn about that in a bit.) Every song or solo we hear is made up of notes from scales. Different scales create different textures or sounds, and the scales we play are directly related to the chords that are played behind them. In other words, certain chord progressions will dictate what scales sound best over them.

It makes sense then, that by practicing scales, we'll be learning the words (or language) of the music. The more words we know, the more eloquently we can speak, or, in the case of music, play. With that in mind, scales make a great practice tool for learning how to improvise. Beyond that, scales also make a great technical workout.

Each scale in this book is presented in standard notation and TAB, as well as a fingerboard diagram. We've included left-hand fingerings between the notation and the TAB—if there's more than one fingering option, we've listed both. (Fingerings are only suggestions, so feel free to experiment and find the solution that works best for you.) In addition, we've listed the note name above each note in the standard notation so you can learn them while working on the scales.

For each scale, there's an audio track that will first, demonstrate the scale played over a chord or chord pattern, then, continue with only the chord accompaniment for you to practice over. After you get comfortable with the scale, I would encourage you to refer to the Appendix. In it, we demonstrate some extra practice ideas—scale sequences and rhythmic variations—that can be applied to every scale. If you're looking to make technique advances, use a metronome to gauge your progress. Always start off playing the scale at a manageable tempo and slowly work your way up to a faster pace. Never sacrifice clarity or precision just to sound faster. Practice doesn't make perfect; practice makes permanent. If you practice with sloppy technique, you will ingrain that into your playing. Challenge yourself with faster tempos, but remember to stay loose and relaxed.

One thing many guitarists are guilty of is simply playing patterns and not knowing the notes. Part of this problem stems from the fact that the guitar is laid out in such a way that playing patterns is very easy, efficient, and understandable. But, you'll be selling yourself short if you simply play patterns instead of actually learning the notes on the fretboard. As I mentioned earlier, all of the scales in the book are labeled with the note names as well, so I encourage you to take the time to study and learn the neck. You won't regret the effort!

With all that being said, let's get into the scales!

OPEN POSITION MAJOR SCALES

C MAJOR

C-D-E-F-G-A-B-C

We'll start off with the C major scale in the open position. "Open position" refers to the use of open strings, as well as notes within the first four frets. C major has no sharps and no flats, so it makes a great starting reference scale. A "major scale" is made up of a series of whole steps (two frets) and half steps (one fret). Looking at our notes, here is the pattern: C - (whole step) - D - (whole step) - E - (half step) - F - (whole step) - G - (whole step) - A - (whole step) - B - (half step) - C. Every major scale shares this pattern (W-W-H-W-W-W-H), but since we start other scales on different notes, we get different spellings for the other major scales. For these major scales, we'll start on the root note (from which we get the name of the scale) and ascend as high as we can within the first four frets.

Visualize It:

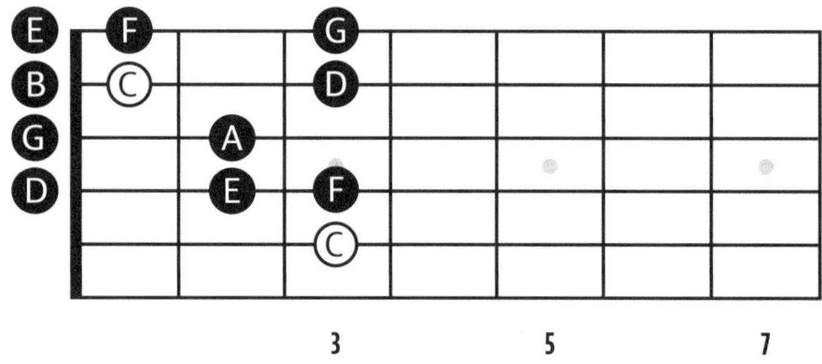

Play It:

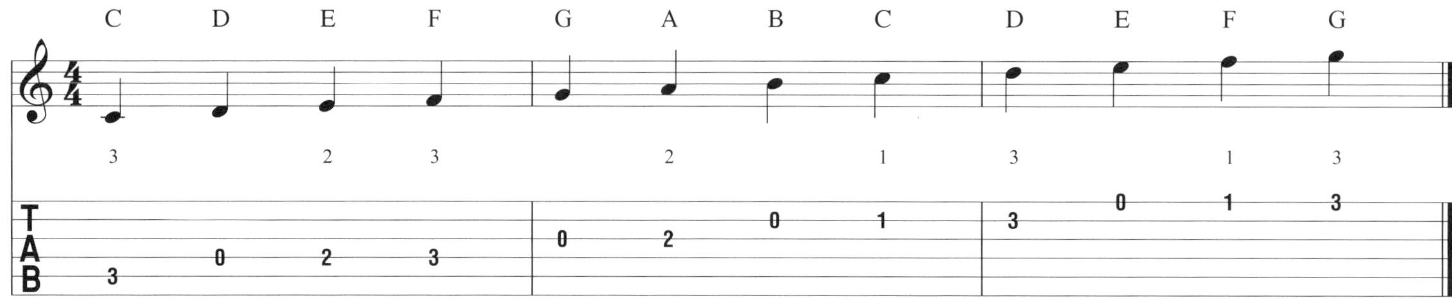

Practice It:

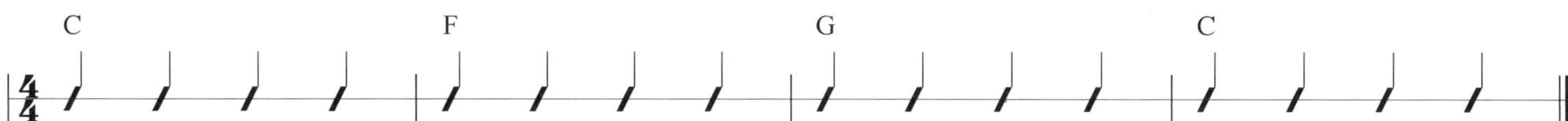

G MAJOR
G-A-B-C-D-E-F♯-G

For the G major scale, notice that the only difference from the C major scale (besides the starting note) is the F♯ note in place of the F natural. In order to preserve our major scale format of whole and half steps, we need to raise the F to an F♯. This pattern will continue as we learn the rest of the major scales, adding sharps (and flats) in order to create more major scale patterns.

Visualize It:

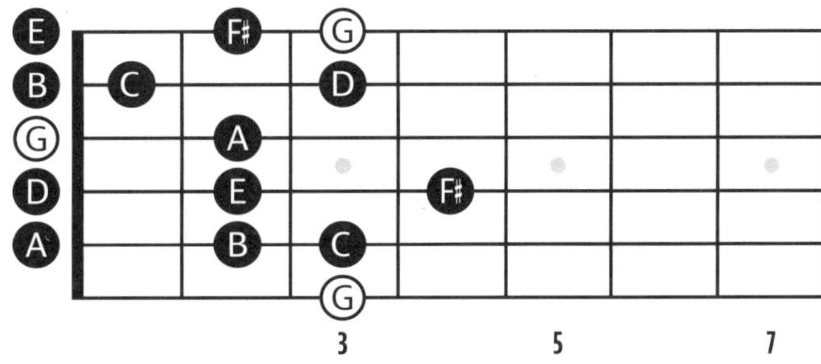

Play It:

Practice It:

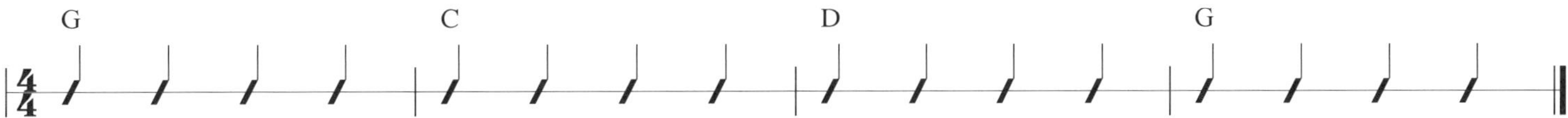

D MAJOR
D-E-F#-G-A-B-C#

For the D major scale, we'll add another sharp, C#. So, now we'll have F# and C#. Notice the pattern here. If we look at C major and then use the 5th note, G, to form a major scale, we have one sharp: F#. Now if we take the 5th note of G major, D, and form a major scale, we have two sharps: F# and C#. Also, notice that C# is five musical letters away from F#. Can you guess what scale is next and what sharp we'll add?

Visualize It:

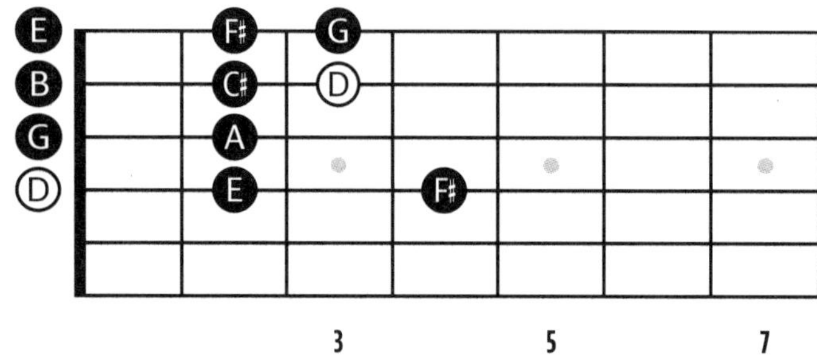

Play It:

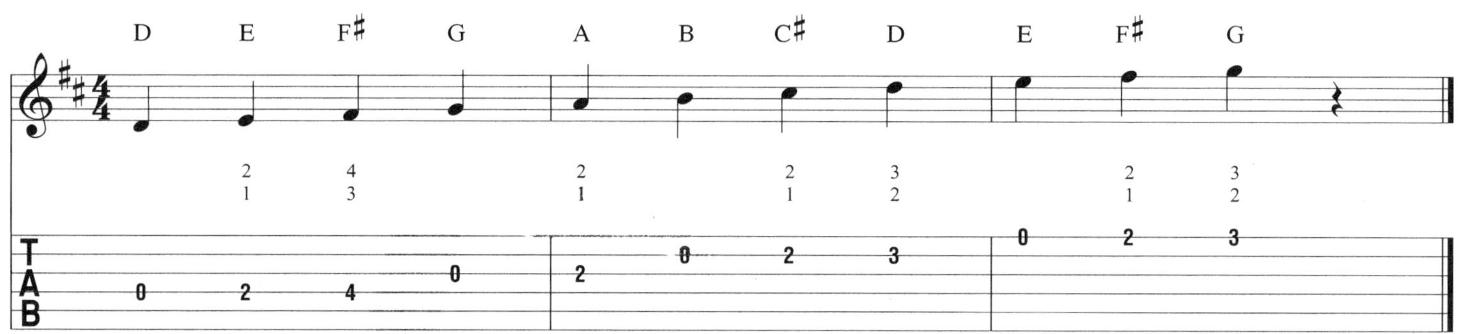

Practice It:

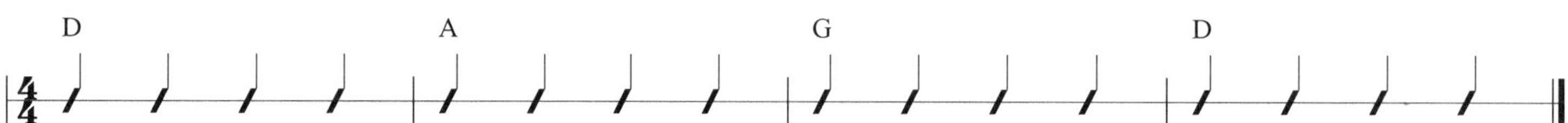

A MAJOR
A-B-C♯-D-E-F♯-G♯

Well, if you guessed A major and adding a G♯, you are correct! This pattern follows the "circle of fifths." In music theory, we use the circle of fifths to help visually organize the 12 tones and memorize the key signatures (the sharps and flats that each major scale has). You'll find this "key signature" written out after the clef sign 𝄞 and before the time signature 4/4. You'll need an understanding of note reading for this to make sense, but that's well worth the effort!

Visualize It:

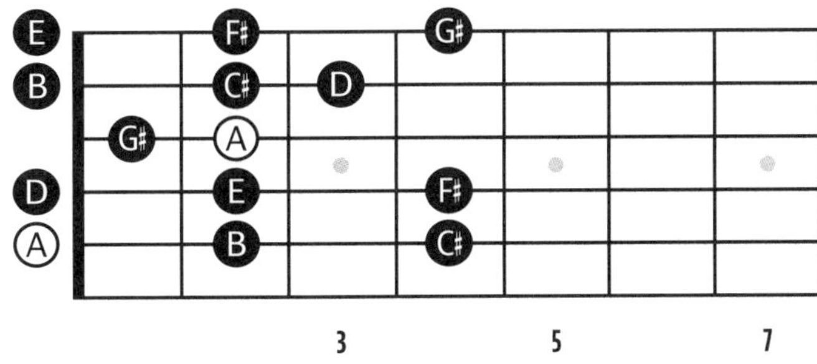

Play It:

Practice It:

E MAJOR
E-F#-G#-A-B-C#-D#

For the E major scale, we'll start on the low sixth string and play all the way up to the G# on the fourth fret of the first string. If you haven't already, this is a great time to start memorizing what the notes are in each scale. Remember, you can always use the circle of fifths to help. As we progress through the circle of fifths, we continue to add sharps, which also follow the circle of fifths pattern. If you're curious about the chords that we're using for the backing track scale practice, these are simply chords that are made up of notes from the scale. They're not the only chords that will work, but they are some of the most common.

Visualize It:

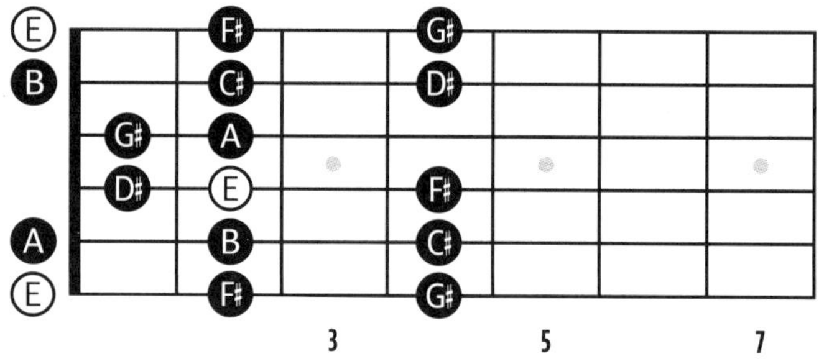

Play It:

Practice It:

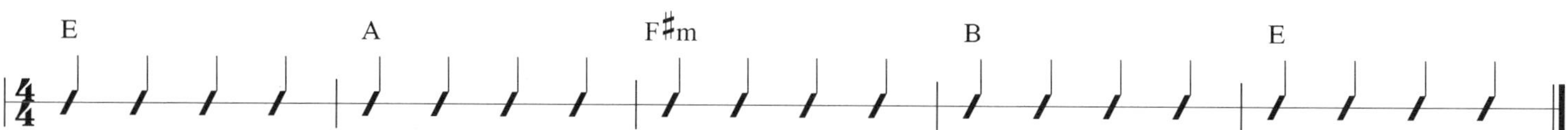

B MAJOR
B-C♯-D♯-E-F♯-G♯-A♯

You can see the sharps are starting to really stack up for the B major scale! Knowing these notes will definitely help your guitar playing and fretboard knowledge. Take your time memorizing them, then try quizzing yourself on spelling out each scale that you've learned so far. While learning the E major scale, we briefly touched on chords. To further explain, we can form a chord on each note of a major scale, and for each scale degree (i.e., 2nd note, 5th note, etc.), the chord quality will always be the same. The first, fourth, and fifth notes will always form major chords; the second, third, and sixth notes will always form minor chords. Using any of those chords in a progression will sound great alongside a melody made up of notes from the corresponding major scale.

Visualize It:

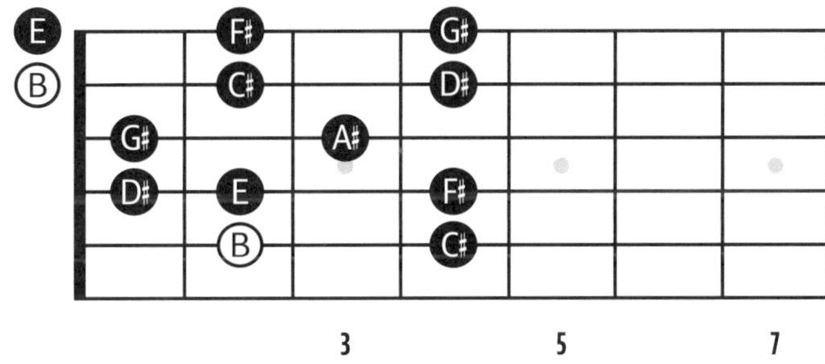

Play It:

Practice It:

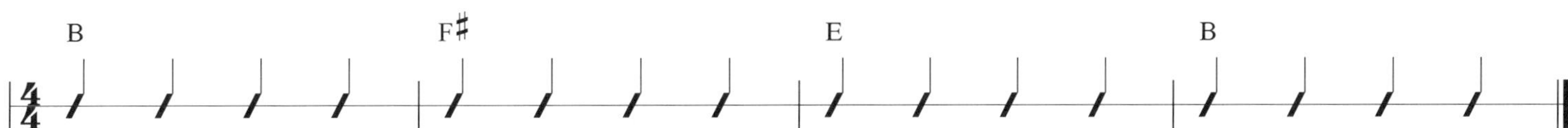

F MAJOR
F-G-A-B♭-C-D-E

Now, let's take a dive into what we call the "flat keys," or scales that have flats in the key signature. Essentially, we're starting over at C again but moving the other direction (counterclockwise) around the circle of fifths—the first stop is the key of F. I find it easier to relate everything to C and view it as "home base." So now, moving through the flat keys, we'll be looking at what the 4th is for the next scale. In the key of C, F is the 4th, and it has one flat, B♭. As we move on, you'll see that determining the flats of the next key can also be found using 4ths.

Visualize It:

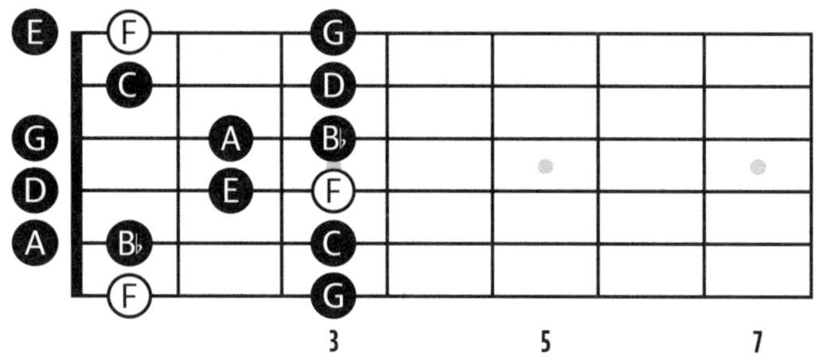

Play It:

Practice It:

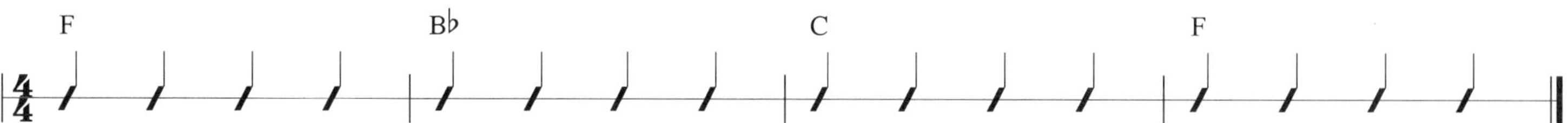

B♭ MAJOR
B♭-C-D-E♭-F-G-A

For the B♭ major scale, we'll have a B♭ and an E♭. Again, notice the pattern: B♭ is the 4th of F, the previous scale we learned. The F major scale had a B♭, and the new flat added (E♭) is the 4th of B♭. There's a reason we're learning the scales in this order. The pattern should help you with memorization. These patterns are great to know, but knowing the notes and formulas for each scale is even better. After practicing the B♭ major scale, can you predict what scale is next?

Visualize It:

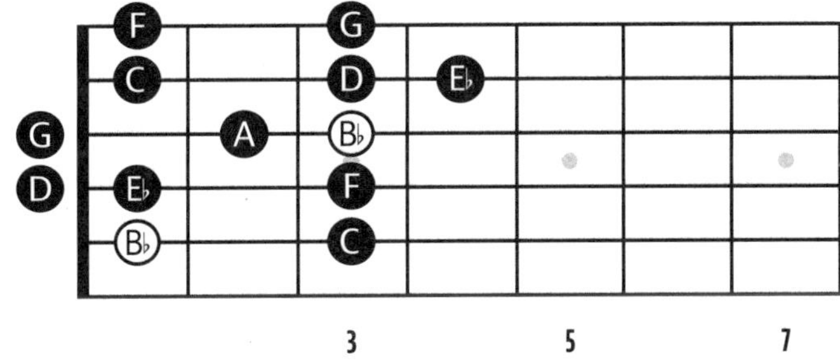

Play It:

Practice It:

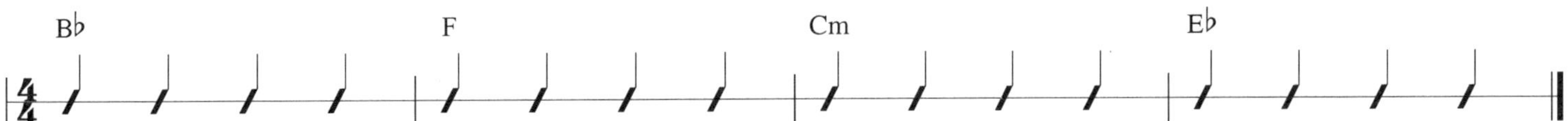

E♭ MAJOR
E♭-F-G-A♭-B♭-C-D

If you guessed E♭ major with three flats, B♭, E♭, and A♭, you are correct! So, not only is scale practice good for technical development, it's also great for composing or learning songs by ear. If you tried to compose a melody without any knowledge of what scale to use, you would fumble with wrong notes and have no real direction. A scale is like a color palette of notes that will sound pleasing with each other. That's not to say that melodies are restricted to notes from a single scale. Indeed, tension can be created using "outside" notes (notes not within the scale). However, in order to use "outside" notes successfully, first we need to know which notes relate well to each other. Additionally, if you're trying to learn a song by ear, knowing what key it's in can give you clues as to what notes or chords might be next.

Visualize It:

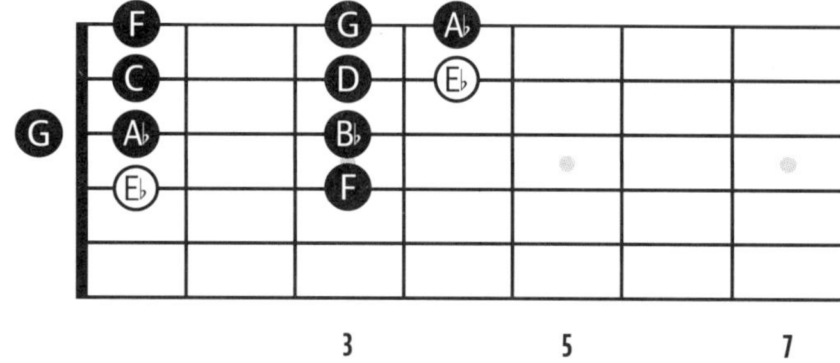

Play It:

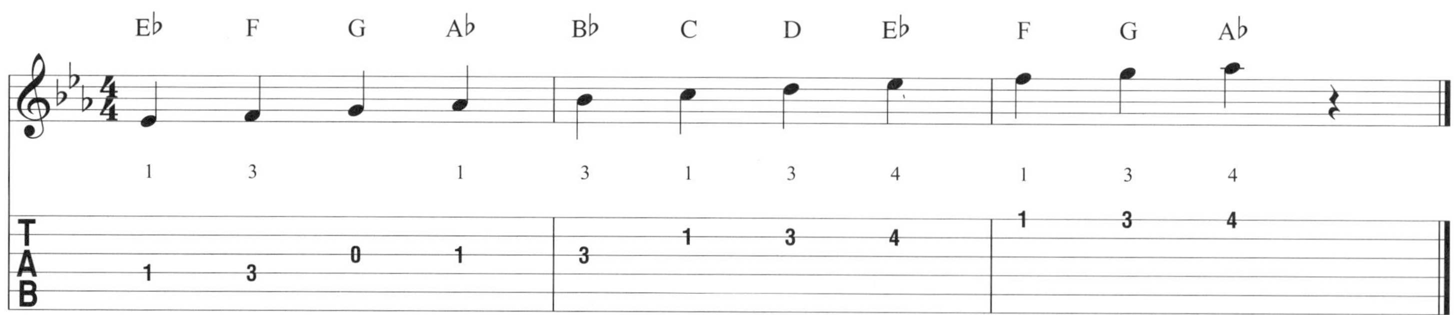

Practice It:

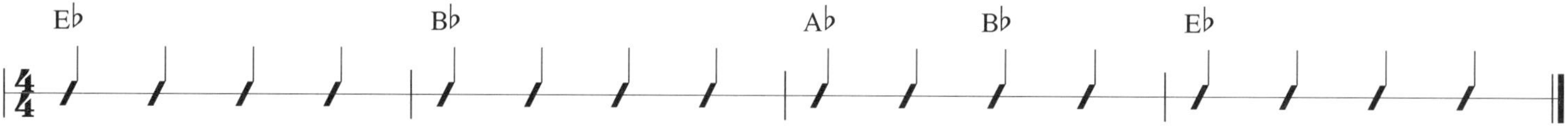

A♭ MAJOR
A♭-B♭-C-D♭-E♭-F-G

For the A♭ major scale, we'll have four flats: B♭, E♭, A♭, and D♭. You might have noticed that we've played some of these notes before, but previously, we referred to them as "sharps." For instance, in the E major scale, we played a D♯ note on the second string, fourth fret. In A♭ major, we have the same second string, fourth fret note, but we call it E♭. So, why do we have essentially the same note but call it a different name? These are called *enharmonic notes*—i.e., notes that have the same pitch but are "spelled" differently. The reason we use enharmonic spellings is because each note name in a major scale can only be used once. In other words, we can't have a D and a D♯. So, instead we call it E♭.

Visualize It:

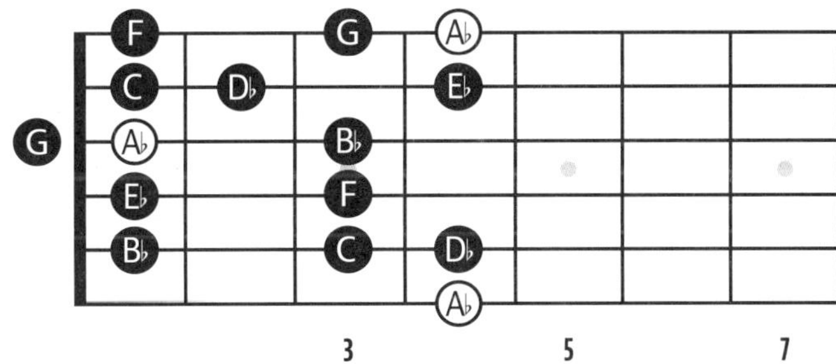

Play It:

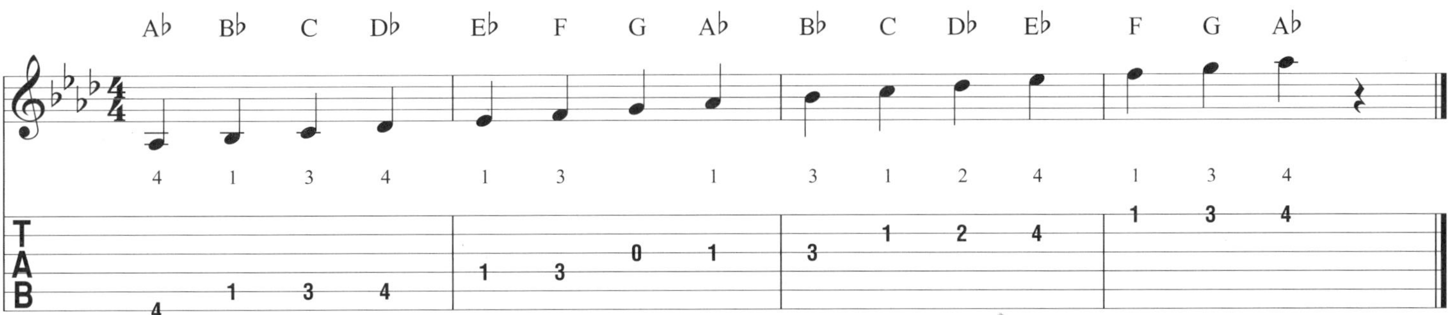

Practice It:

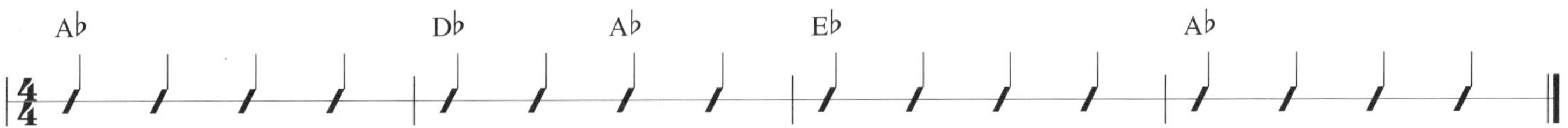

D♭ MAJOR
D♭-E♭-F-G♭-A♭-B♭-C

You might be wondering, why bother learning all these flat keys when almost everything you play is typically in a sharp key (G, D, A, E)? True, most guitar-based tunes will usually be in a key that features sharps, because that makes better use of open-string notes and open chords. However, if you venture into playing any jazz or show tunes, or even some songs written for piano, you'll find many are in the flat keys (especially in jazz). It's always a great idea to be well rounded! So, let's go practice our D♭ major scale.

Visualize It:

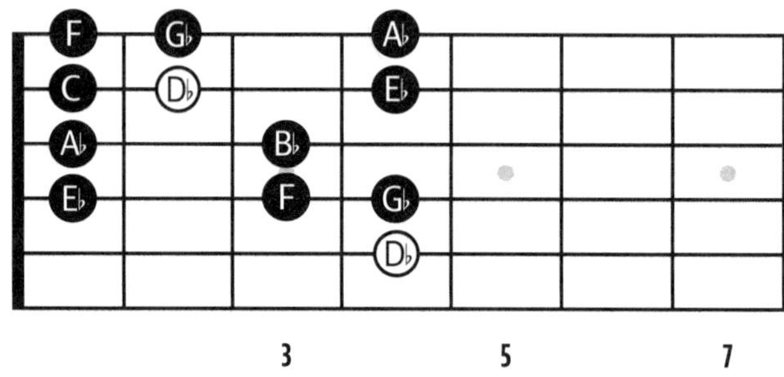

Play It:

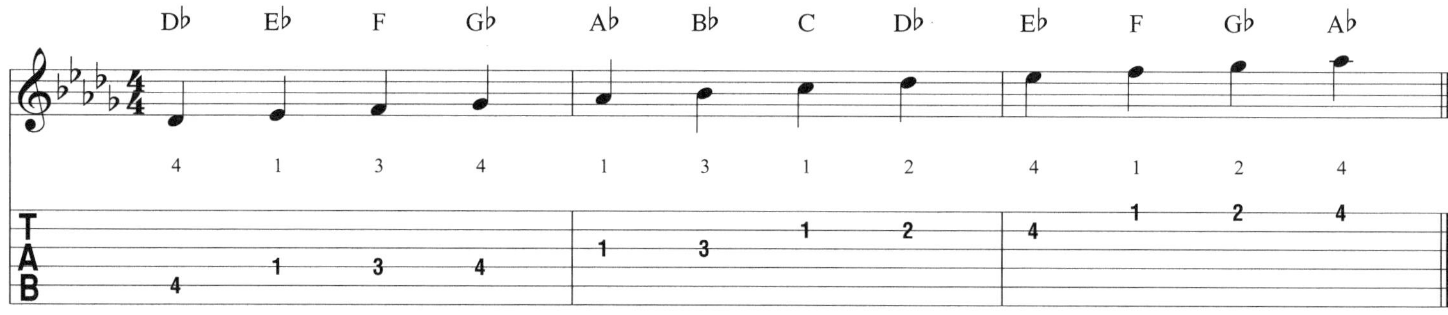

Practice It:

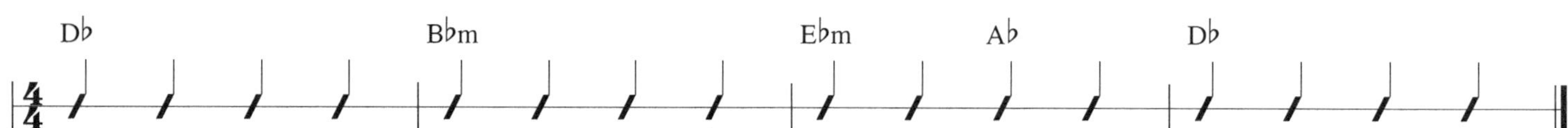

F♯ MAJOR
F♯-G♯-A♯-B-C♯-D♯-E♯

So, here we have our final major scale: F♯ major. You might be wondering why it's not called Gb major? Well, it could be; in fact, there are a few "enharmonic scales." F♯ major, with six sharps, could also be G♭ major, with six flats (B♭, E♭, A♭, D♭, G♭, C♭). The other two enharmonic scales are D♭/C♯ and B/C♭. In the case of Db major, we have five flats as opposed to the enharmonic C♯ major with seven sharps: C♯-D♯-E♯-F♯-G♯-A♯-B♯. Yes, you read that correctly; every note is sharp! Finally, for B major, we have five sharps, whereas the enharmonic C♭ has seven flats: C♭-D♭-E♭-F♭-G♭-A♭-B♭. (Every note is flat.)

Visualize It:

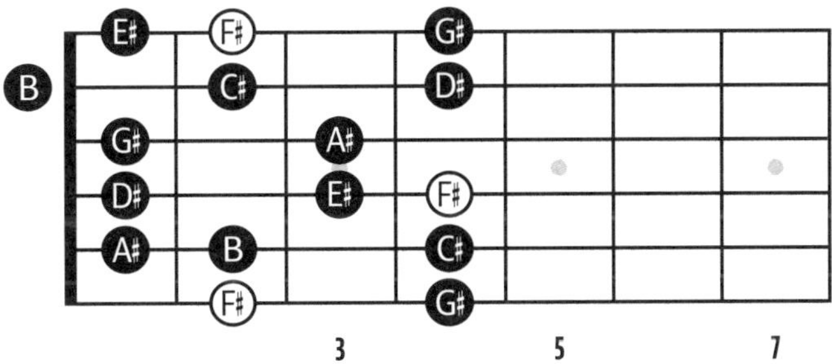

Play It:

Practice It:

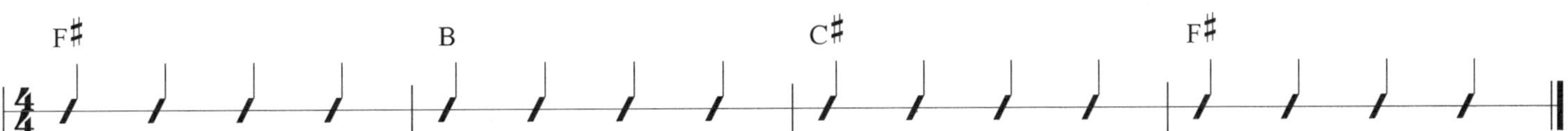

PENTATONIC SCALES

E MINOR PENTATONIC - OPEN POSITION

E-G-A-B-D

All the major scales we learned so far have seven notes. In comparison, the E minor pentatonic scale contains just five notes. Pentatonic scales are extremely popular with guitarists, as they lay out very nicely on the fretboard and are great for improvising. The E minor pentatonic comes from the E minor scale with the 2nd and 6th notes omitted. (Don't worry, we'll be learning full minor scales a little later on.) By omitting the 2nd and 6th note, every note will sound good when played over a chord progression in a given key.

Visualize It:

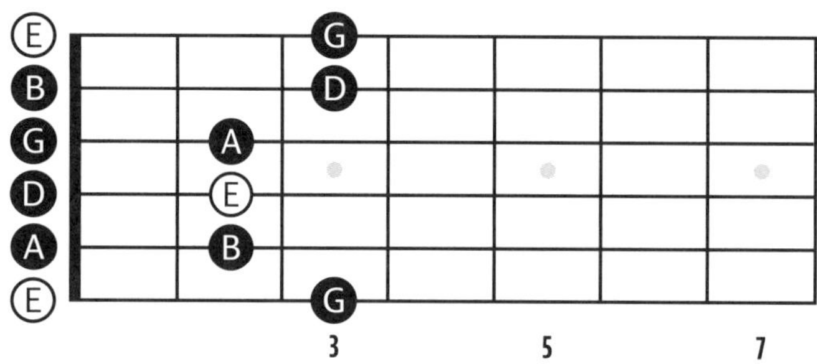

Play It:

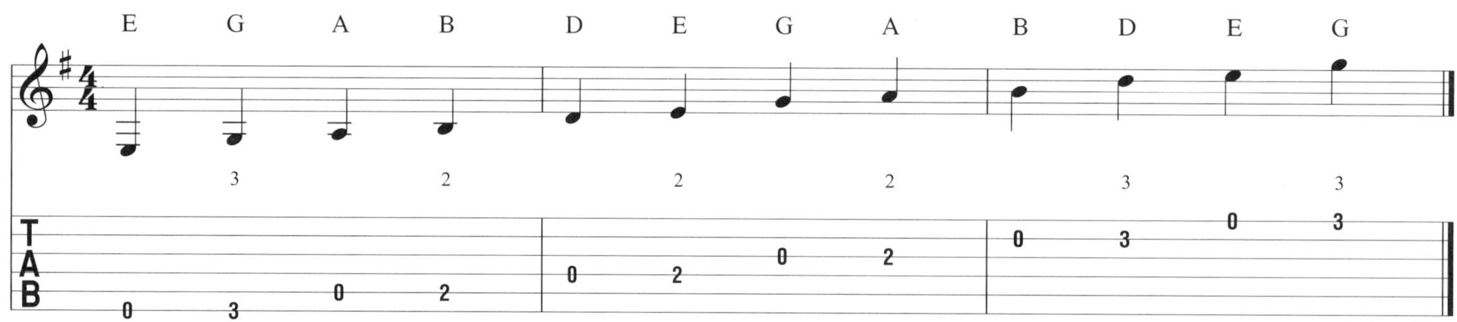

Practice It:

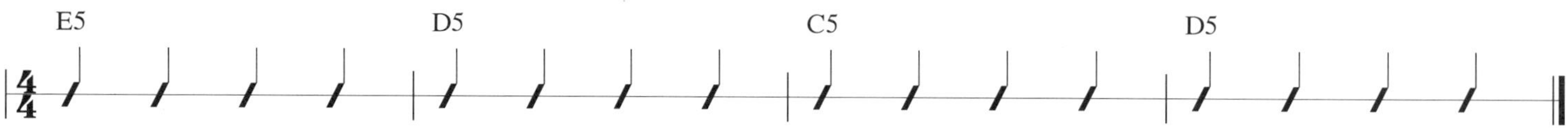

A MINOR PENTATONIC - POSITION #1
A-C-D-E-G

The A minor pentatonic just might be the most used scale in the history of guitar. From early rock and roll, all the way to modern heavy metal, this scale sees a lot of use among all players. Notice that it is the same shape that we used in the previous E minor pentatonic scale. We simply moved everything up five frets, including those open strings. This is where the guitar has an advantage over other instruments like piano or saxophone—we can take one scale and, by keeping the same shape, get a new key just by moving it around the neck. We'll explore this idea more in future scales, but for now, get this iconic scale under your fingers. This is the "home base" pattern for this scale, which we'll call "Position #1."

Visualize It:

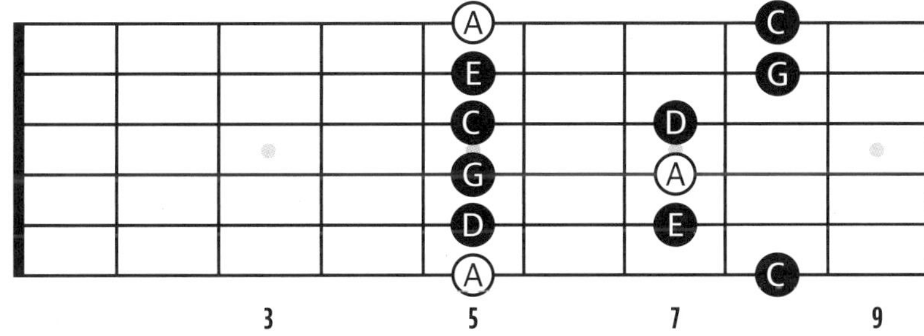

Play It:

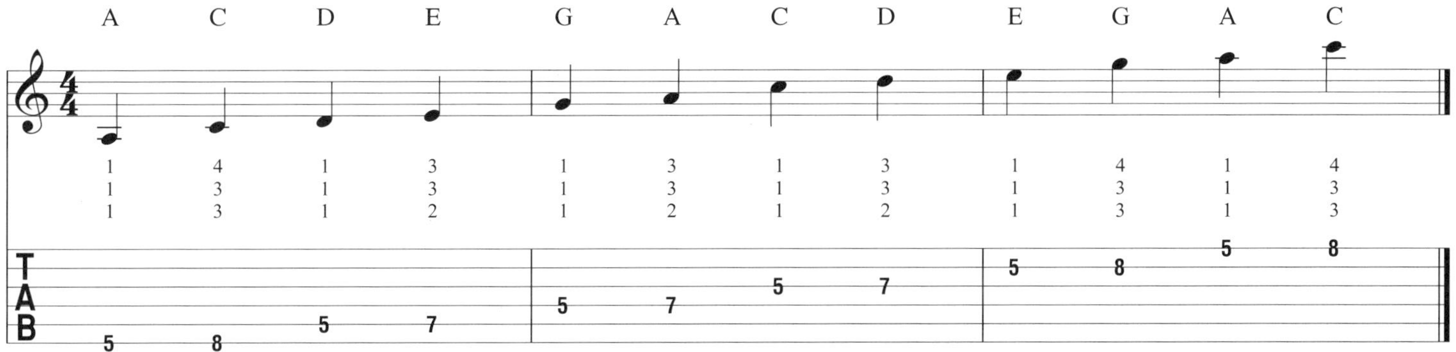

Practice It:

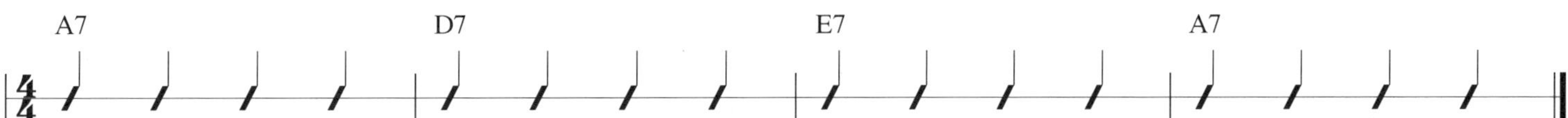

A MINOR PENTATONIC - SLIDING
A-C-D-E-G

Using the same notes, we can play the A minor pentatonic in a different way: diagonally across the neck as opposed to vertically. This will allow us to add some higher notes as well as simplifying the fingering. Notice we use only the first and third fingers, with the third finger doing some position slides. This form might be a little harder to memorize as it's not as compact on the fretboard. Challenge yourself to play it ascending and descending and even try starting on notes in the middle of the scale. Remember, when improvising, you don't want to have to rely on playing the scale from the root or starting note. You'll want to have command of that scale starting on any string. This will take time, so be patient.

Visualize It:

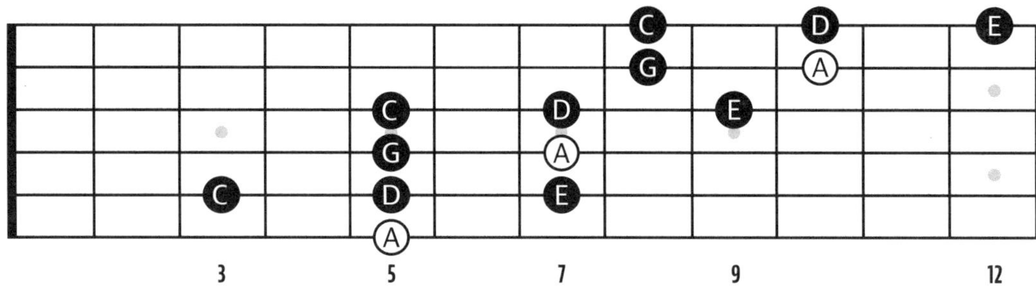

Play It:

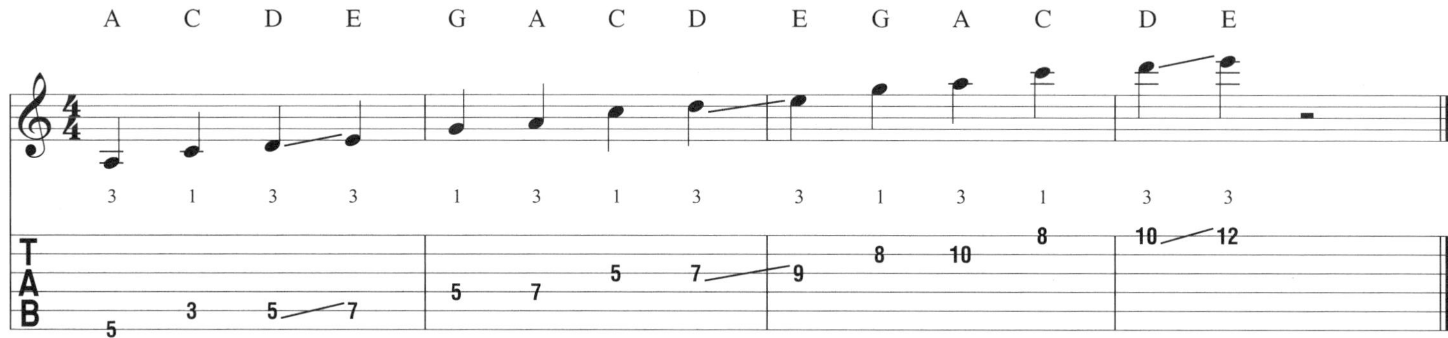

Practice It:

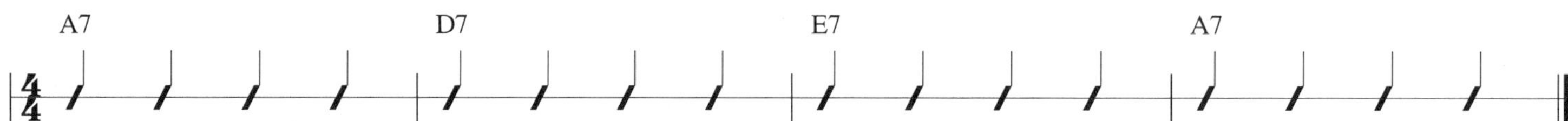

A MINOR PENTATONIC - POSITION #2
A-C-D-E-G

We can also take the same notes of the A minor pentatonic and play them in a different position with a different starting note. Again, the key here is that you don't want to just think of these scales as a pattern with a starting note, but rather a system of notes all over the neck. In other words, if you want to start a melody or solo on the A note at the second string, tenth fret, you don't want to have to start your scale on the sixth string just to find the pattern. Visualize the entire scale on all strings and, again, challenge yourself to start from any note of the scale. It can help to know the root notes, so even though the scale starts on C on the sixth string, our root note is still A. It is good then to anchor this position with either the A on the fourth string or the A on the second string.

Visualize It:

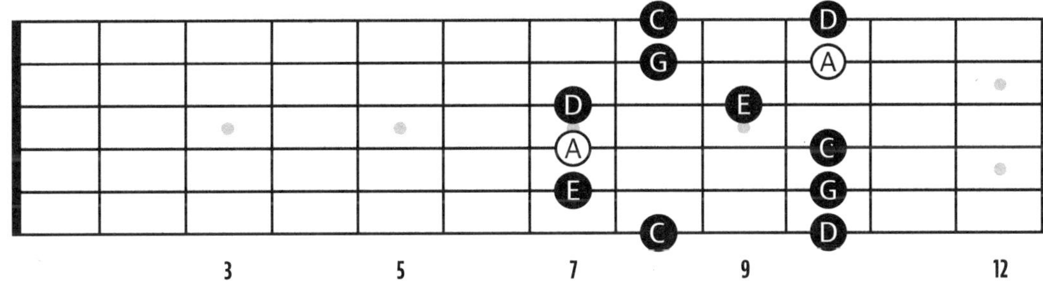

Play It:

Practice It:

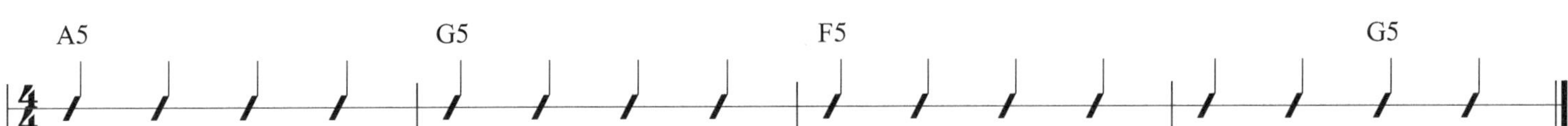

A MINOR PENTATONIC - POSITION #3
A-C-D-E-G

As you learn this new position of the A minor pentatonic scale, challenge yourself to go back to the previous two positions and connect them. Start anywhere within the scale and see if you can meander back to the other two positions. By doing this, you can see that the diagonal version we learned contains all of the notes of the first three positions. Having the ability to play the same note on different strings can make the guitar both easier and, at the same time, more difficult to learn. Always remember: don't just think about the patterns. Learn those note names!

Visualize It:

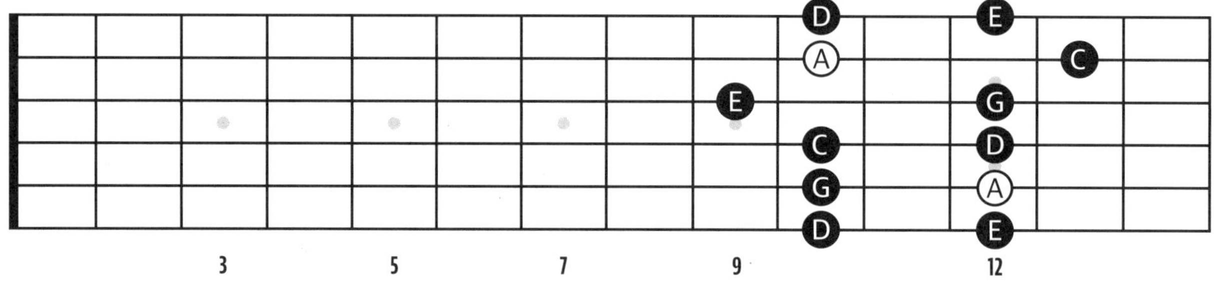

Play It:

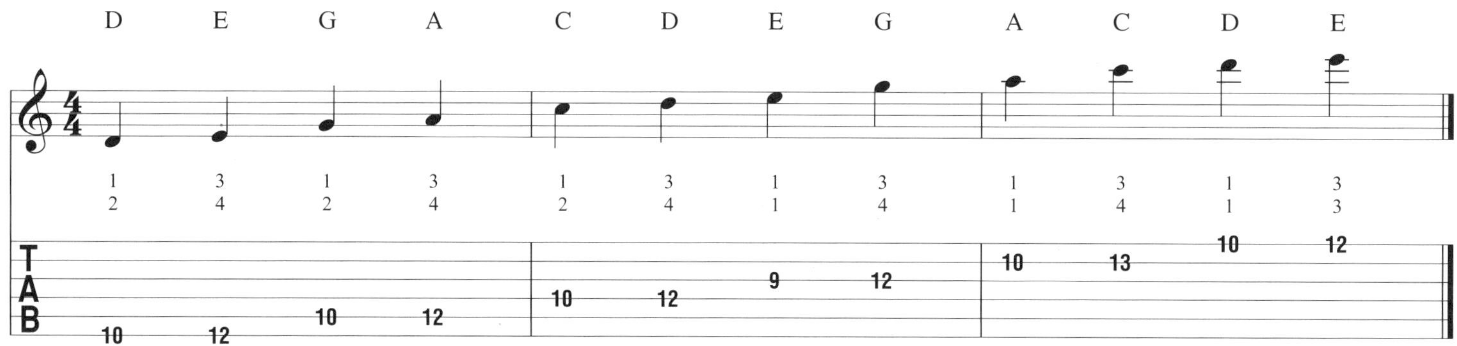

Practice It:

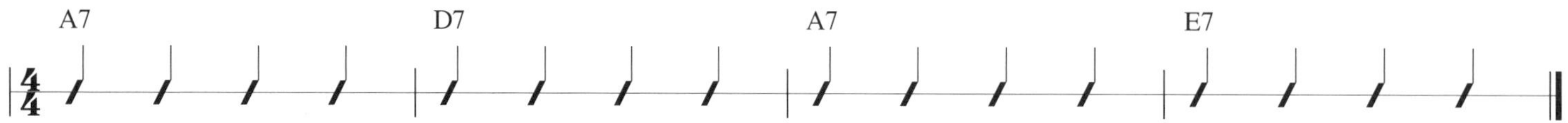

A MINOR PENTATONIC - POSITION #4
A-C-D-E-G

Here's A minor pentatonic in position #4. Again, just to be clear, all these positions contain the same notes in the same order. We're just starting and ending the pattern on a different note each time. So, it's not a new or different scale; we're simply playing the notes of the scale in a different location on the fretboard. As you can see, we're getting higher up the neck, so this position is giving us some great choices for soloing.

Visualize It:

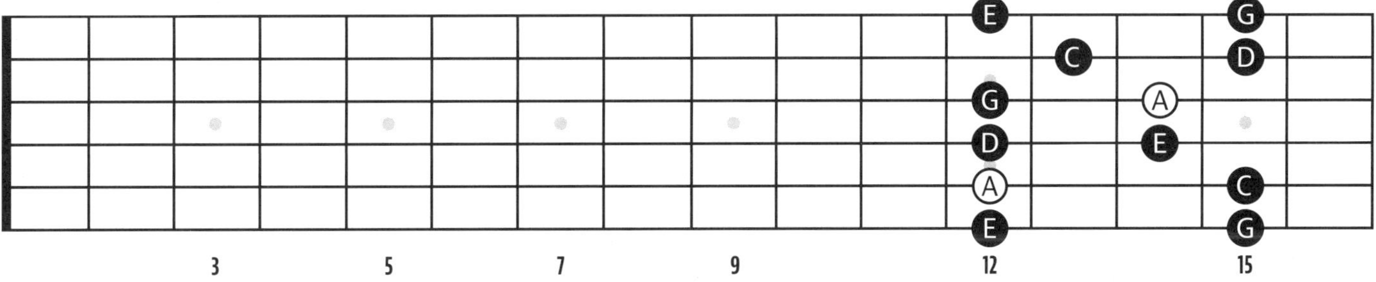

Play It:

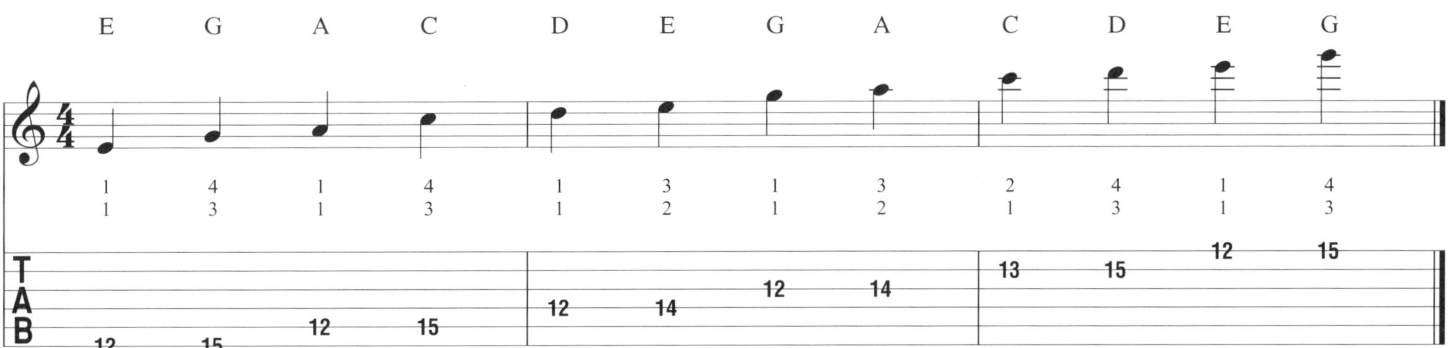

Practice It:

A MINOR PENTATONIC - POSITION #5
A-C-D-E-G

For the final A minor pentatonic position, we'll take a look at two options: one starting on the third fret and the other starting an octave higher on the 15th fret. These two positions have the same exact notes, but they're played in two different octaves. It's a very symmetrical shape, so it should be easy to memorize. We'll touch on this topic more, but all of these pentatonic patterns are *movable*. That means we can take this same shape, move it up a fret, and get a completely different key. Just pay attention to what the root note is—A, in this case—as it will name the key. For example, if we start this pattern on the seventh fret (two frets higher), that will make the root note a B instead of an A, so the new scale would be a B minor pentatonic. We'll go into more detail later in the book on this, but for now, try and understand that these shapes can be played all over the neck yielding different keys. That's important, because you won't only be soloing or creating melodies in A minor!

Visualize It:

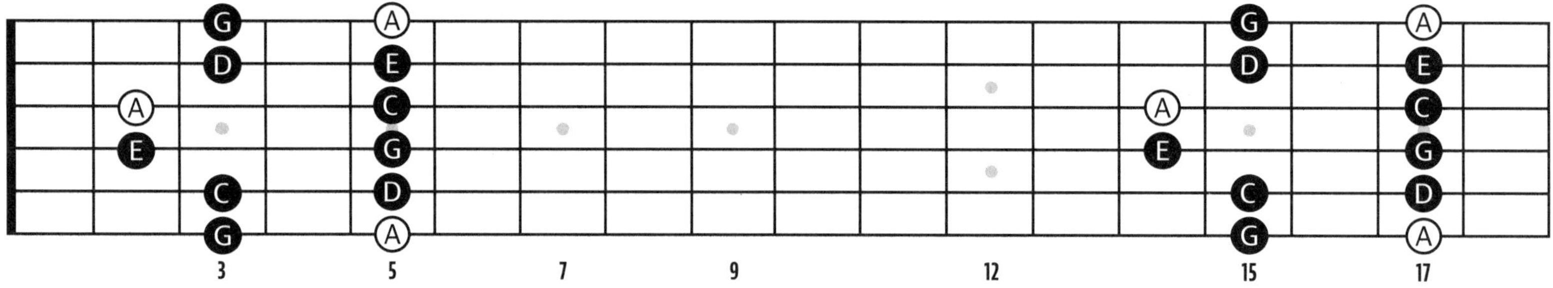

Play It:

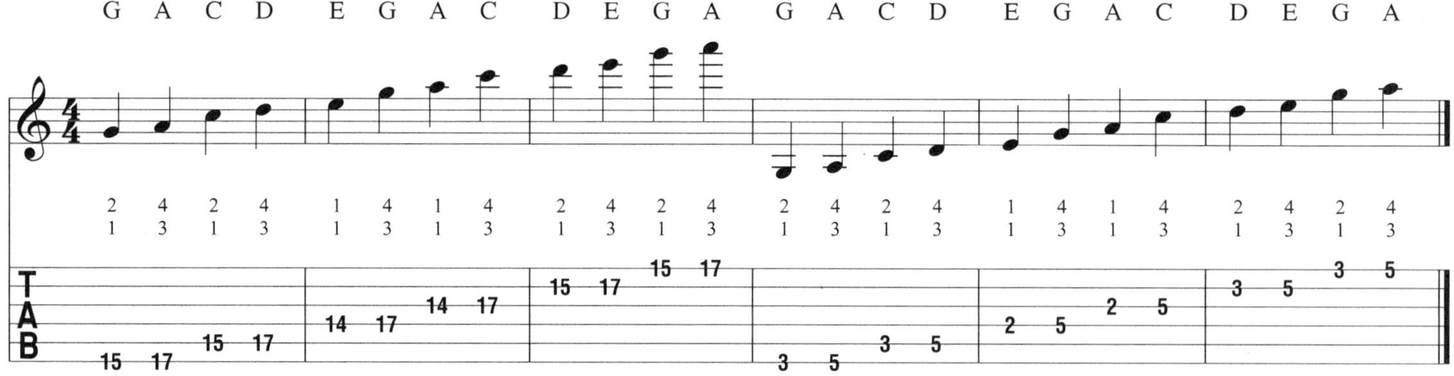

Practice It:

A BLUES SCALE
A-C-D-E♭-E-G

The A blues scale is simply an A minor pentatonic with one added note: an E♭, or ♭5th. This flatted 5th is what gives the scale a bluesy flavor. It's widely used for soloing over blues progressions and other genres, including rock, jazz, and country. We're learning the scale here in the most common position. Just as we did with the pentatonic scales, however, we can plot these notes all over the guitar as well. I would encourage you to get familiar with the blues scale in those same positions we learned for the minor pentatonic. It's just one added note, so if you have a handle on those other scales, you'll just need to be aware of where the "blue note" is.

Visualize It:

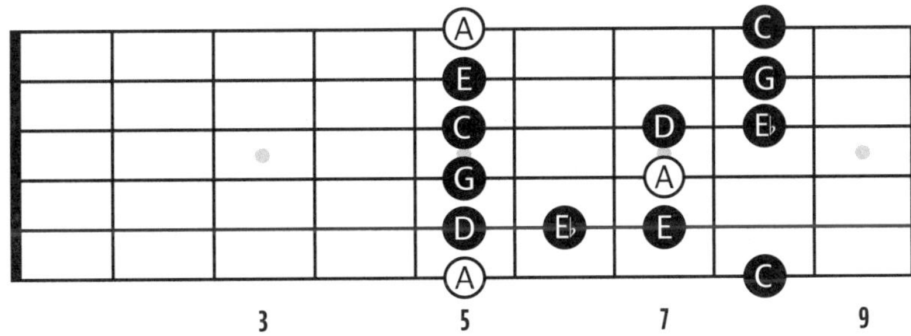

Play It:

Practice It:

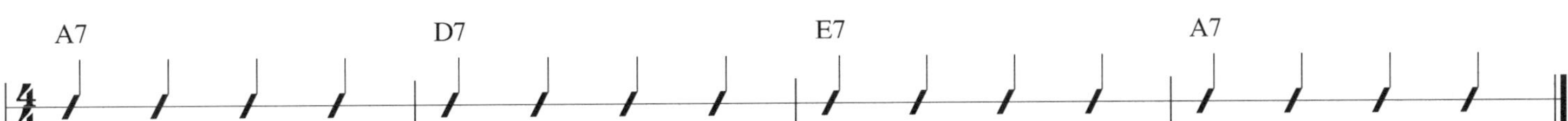

A MINOR PENTATONIC WITH MAJOR 6TH

A-C-D-E-F♯

By replacing the 7th tone of the minor scale with the major 6th, we get a nice variation for the pentatonic scale. Normally, our 6th tone (from the A minor scale) would be F, but if we make that a major interval, we get F♯. Intervals are simply the difference in pitch between two notes. We describe intervals with numbers that relate to their distance from the root note. In other words, if we look at what's in an A major scale, the 6th note would be F♯. We'll get a little deeper into intervals later in the book, but for now, let's look at what makes this scale work. When played over a blues progression, that F♯ brings out the 3rd of the D7 or, as it's called in the blues, the "IV chord." Bringing this note out will add a smooth, jazzy, and sweet flavor. Once you learn the scale, practice over the backing track, switching between this new scale and the A minor pentatonic to really hear the difference. If you'd like to hear this scale in action, check out Robben Ford or Joe Bonamassa.

Visualize It:

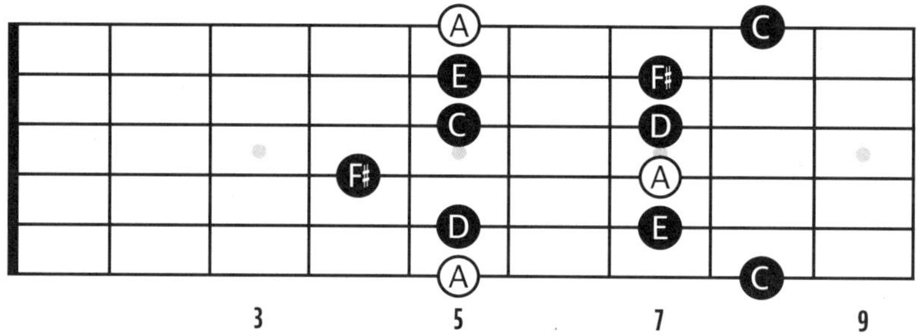

Play It:

Practice It:

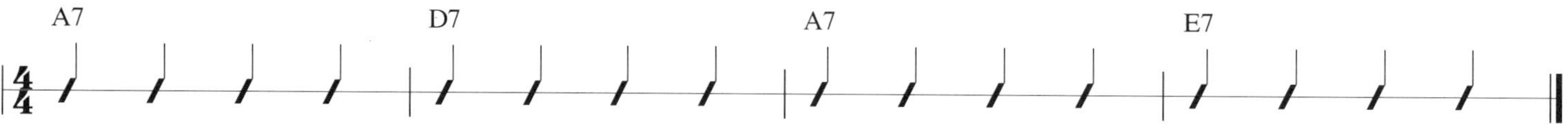

A MAJOR PENTATONIC - POSITION #1
A-B-C♯-E-F♯

Just like we can build a five-note pentatonic scale from the minor scale, we can do the same with the major scale. These five notes are pulled from the A major scale and contain the following intervals: 1-2-3-5-6 (the 4th and 7th degrees are omitted). In general, you'll find the major pentatonic sounds great over any major chord progression. In other words, if a song is in the key of A major, then the A major pentatonic will sound great. You can also use the major pentatonic over a blues progression, yielding a much sweeter or "happier" sound than the typical bluesy sound of the minor pentatonic. In fact, many blues players will switch back and forth between the two scales, often times playing the same licks but using the different scales. Try switching between the major and minor pentatonic over the backing track to hear the difference.

Visualize It:

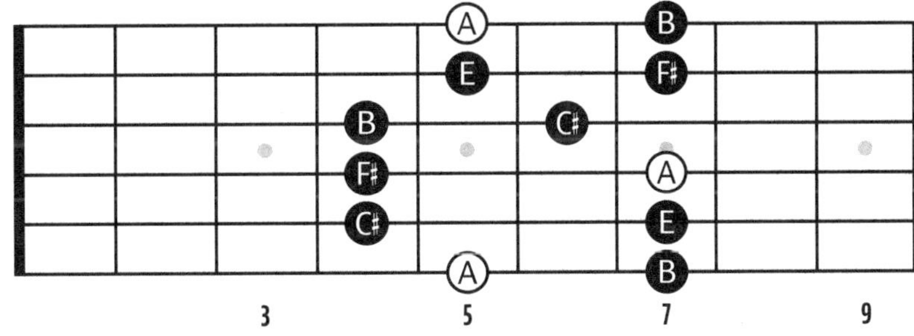

Play It:

Practice It:

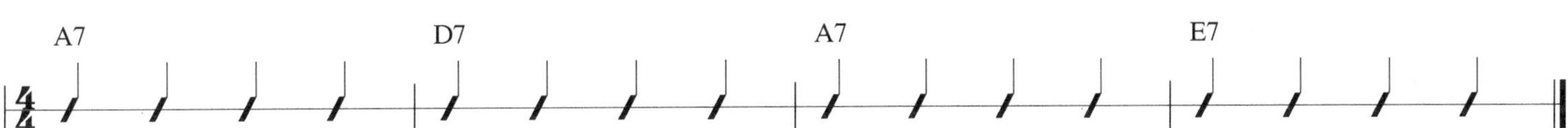

A MAJOR PENTATONIC - POSITION #2
A-B-C♯-E-F♯

Just like we did with the minor pentatonic, we'll be learning the major pentatonic in different positions all over the neck. To clarify again, playing the A major pentatonic in this second position will still yield the same notes as the first position we learned previously. In addition, you would still use it over the same A major chord progression. Don't confuse this with different keys. Playing in a different key would mean taking the same scale shape and moving it to different frets. For example, this position of the A major scale starts on the seventh fret. If you took this same shape and moved it up two frets, then you would have a B major pentatonic scale—we'll be doing more of that later. For now, because pentatonic scales are so widely used and popular with guitar, the most important thing is learning all the different positions within a single key.

Visualize It:

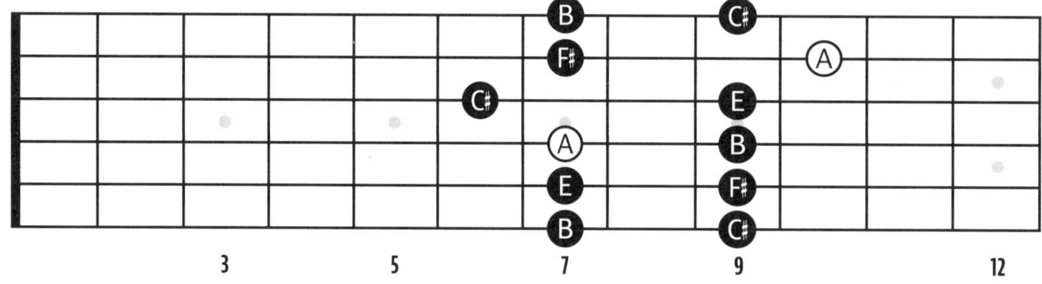

Play It:

Practice It:

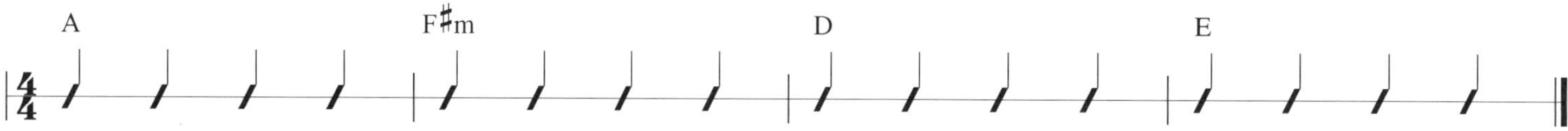

A MAJOR PENTATONIC - POSITION #3
A-B-C♯-E-F♯

Again, as you learn each new pentatonic position, try and connect it to the previous position. The goal is to have seamless integration of all the pentatonic positions all over the neck. Remember to anchor the scale by the root note. In this case, use the A on the fifth string, 12th fret. Try and visualize the shape or pattern of the scale based on that root note. Then, do some experimenting and see if you can play it in other keys. Try and find it in the key of G (10th fret) or D (fifth fret). All you need to do is find the root note on the fifth string and then play the scale shape. If you're having trouble locating the root note, it's time to put in some more effort into knowing the notes on the fingerboard!

Visualize It:

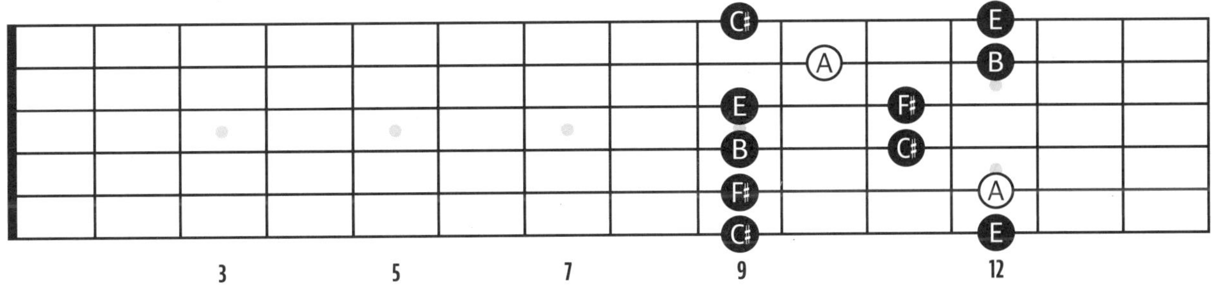

Play It:

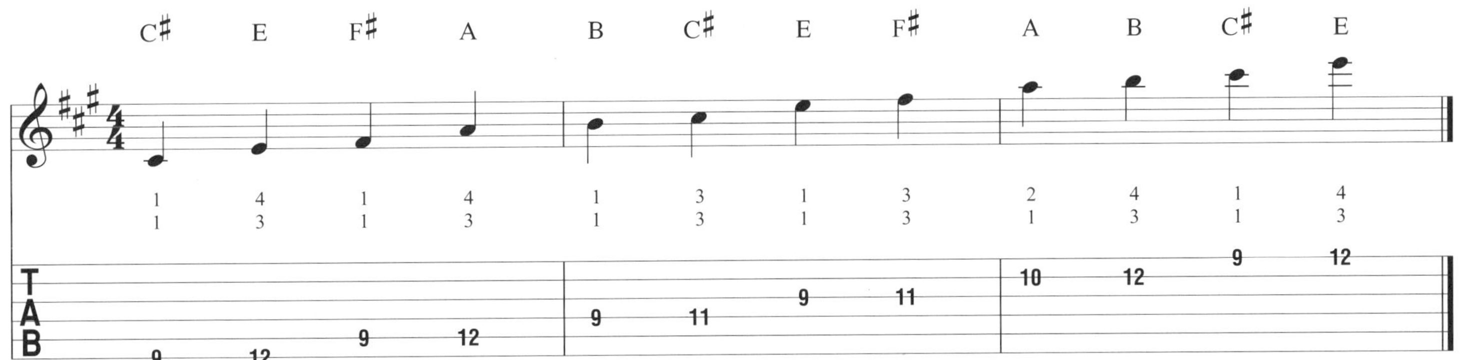

Practice It:

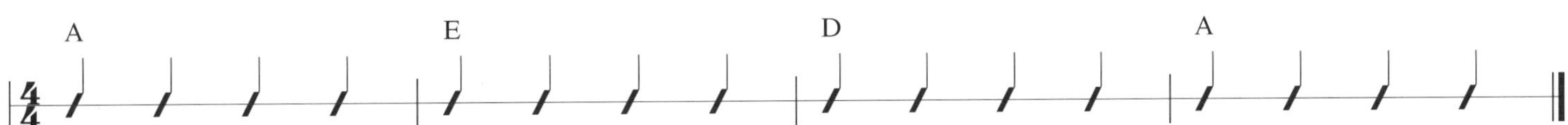

A MAJOR PENTATONIC - POSITION #4
A-B-C♯-E-F♯

This is the most symmetrical of all the positions so the shape should be rather easy to memorize. Once memorized, it's a good time to go ahead and connect the four major pentatonic shapes you've leaned so far. As you go through them, don't neglect learning those note names. Knowing the note names of the frets on the guitar will be a huge help and will also further cement the note names of each scale. Much like technical skill on the guitar, it will take repeated practice to get the note names down. Stick with it and don't get discouraged if you forget some notes. That is part of the process and will eventually make the connections stronger.

Visualize It:

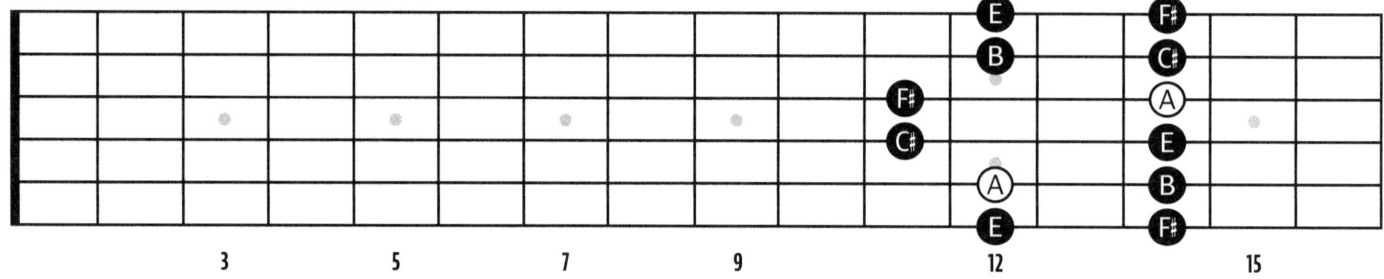

Play It:

Practice It:

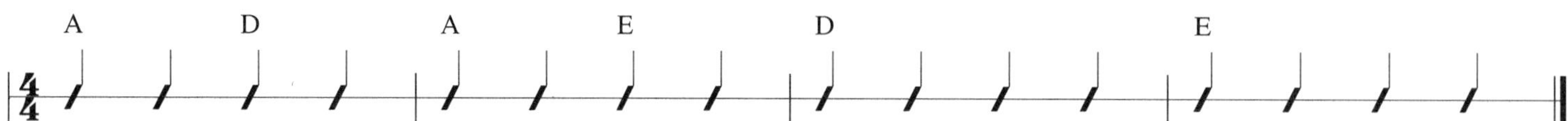

A MAJOR PENTATONIC - POSITION #5
A-B-C♯-E-F♯

For our final position of the major pentatonic, we'll offer two options that are one octave apart. At this point, hopefully you've noticed the connection between the major pentatonic positions with the minor pentatonic positions. If not, the connection is that the major pentatonic contains the same notes as the minor pentatonic that is three frets lower. In other words, if you play notes from the A *major pentatonic*, you're also playing notes from the F♯ *minor pentatonic*. This relationship is called "relative major and minor." For any major scale, the relative minor is built on the 6th degree. Both scales will have the same notes but will have different starting root notes. The C major scale starts on C; its relative minor, the A minor scale, starts on A. You might be asking, "If they're basically the same, do I have to know both?" The answer is yes and no. It's good to have a solid understanding of all the scales in their own right. However, it saves some time and effort to remember the relative major/minor relationship, because the scale patterns we learned for the minor positions show up again as major scale positions, and vice versa. Most importantly, if you know what notes to play in a given key, you're good to go.

Visualize It:

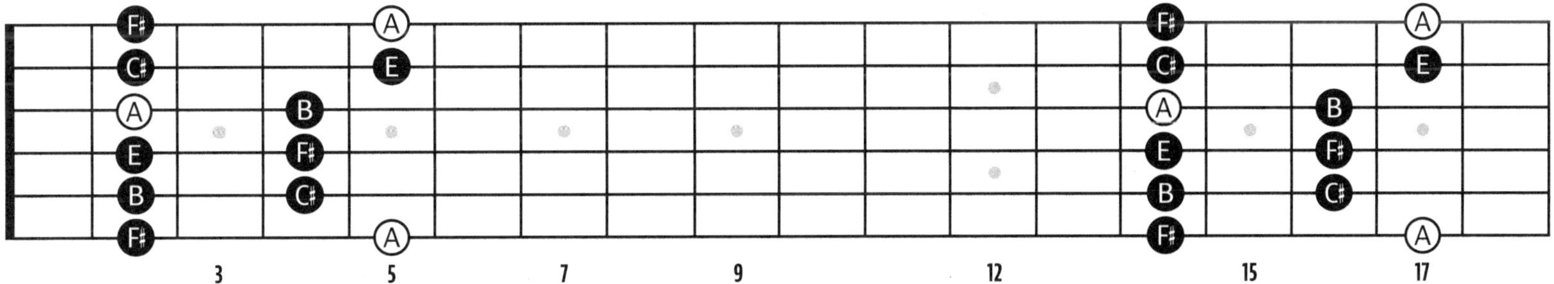

Play It:

Practice It:

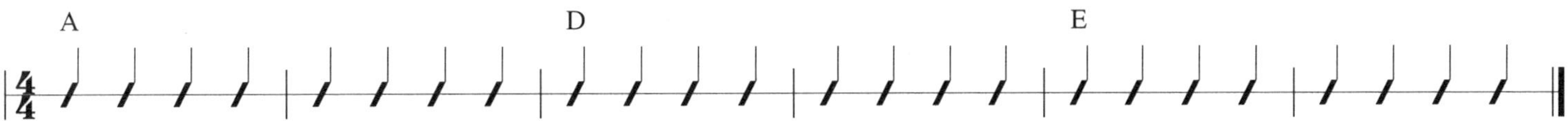

MINOR SCALES

A MINOR

A-B-C-D-E-F-G

Now that we've learned about relative major and minor scales, let's learn the A minor scale, or A natural minor, as it is also called. Again, the A minor scale will have exactly the same notes as the C major scale; in practical terms, they are the same scale. But, to understand the music theory behind them, we look at these scales differently. We briefly discussed intervals before when we defined them as the distance between two notes. In the case of A minor, the "A," or root, is the 6th interval of the C major scale. Intervals not only have a number, but also a quality. The five types or "qualities" of intervals are major, perfect, minor, augmented, and diminished. Within a major scale, you'll only have major and perfect intervals. The major intervals will be the 2nd, 3rd, 6th, and 7th, while the 4th and 5th will be perfect intervals. In comparison, for a minor scale, we'll have a major 2nd, a perfect 4th and 5th, and minor intervals for the 3rd, 6th, and 7th. To make it easier to understand, a minor interval is simply a major interval lowered by one half step (one fret). So, for example, A to C# is a major 3rd interval, while A to C is a minor 3rd. We'll discuss more throughout the book, but try and digest this much while you learn the A minor scale.

Visualize It:

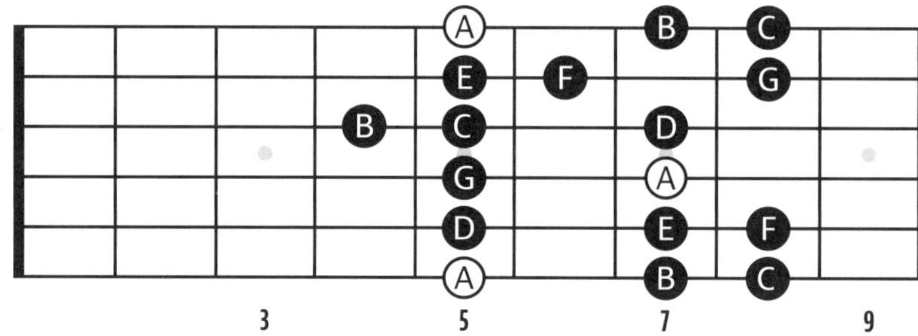

Play It:

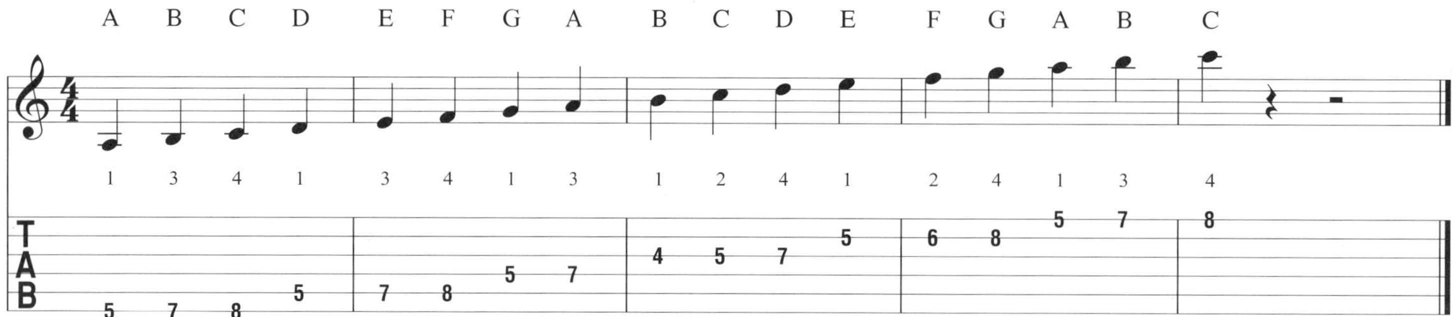

Practice It:

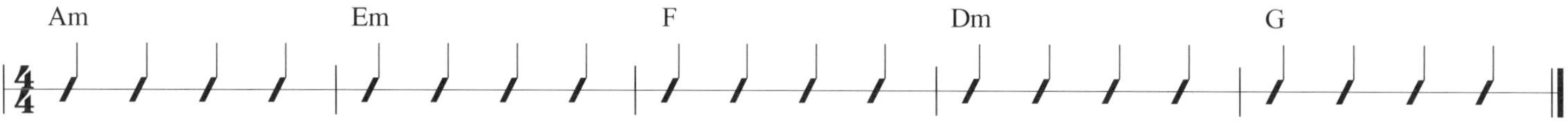

A MELODIC MINOR
A-B-C-D-E-F♯-G♯

The melodic minor scale differs from the natural minor in that the 6th and 7th tones are raised by one half step, or one fret. It's used frequently in jazz and also in classical music. When used in classical music, it is odd in the fact that it ascends using the melodic minor notes and descends using the natural minor notes. For jazz, we use the same scale—with the raised 6th and 7th—in both directions. This scale might twist your ear a bit and take some getting used to, as the notes aren't all from a standard major or minor scale. But, that bit of tension is what makes music interesting and, additionally, makes resolutions that much stronger. To hear the melodic minor scale in action, check out the second measure of The Beatles' "Yesterday" ("I'm not half the man I used to be") as well as the popular Christmas song "Carol of the Bells."

Visualize It:

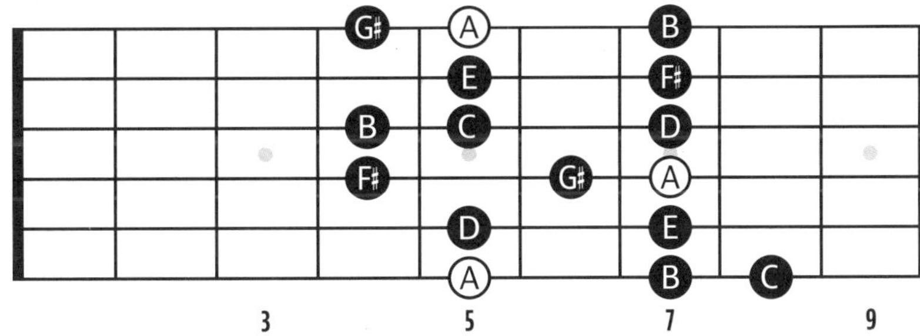

Play It:

Practice It:

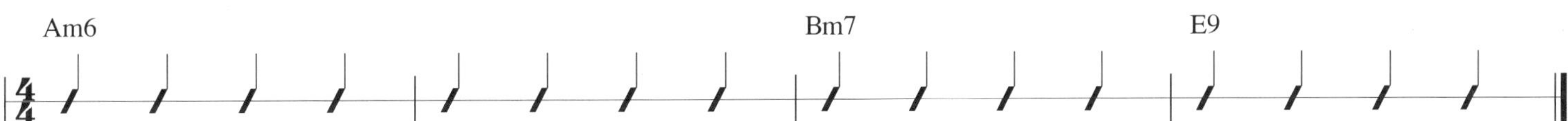

A HARMONIC MINOR
A-B-C-D-E-F-G♯

The only difference between the natural minor and the harmonic minor is the raised 7th degree, but that one change makes a huge difference! This scale has been used extensively in classical music as well as in Spanish and Flamenco music. When improvising, it works well over a dominant 7th chord that is resolving to a minor chord. Take a look at our example: E7 to Am. For some applications in popular music, listen to Dire Straits "Sultans of Swing." Also, check out the guitar work of Yngwie Malmsteen, Randy Rhoads, or Richie Blackmore, as they all made great use of the harmonic minor scale when soloing.

Visualize It:

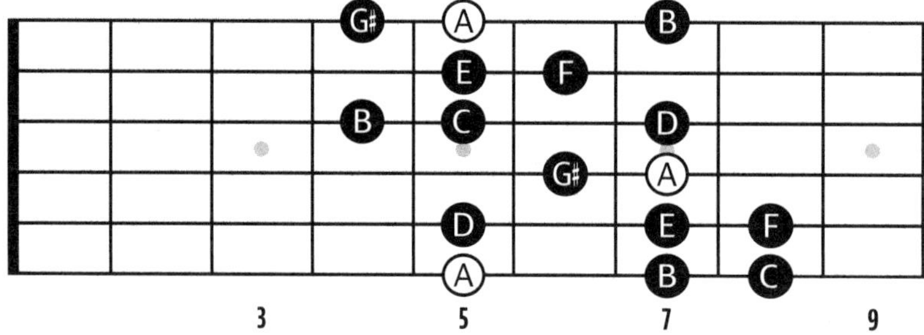

Play It:

Practice It:

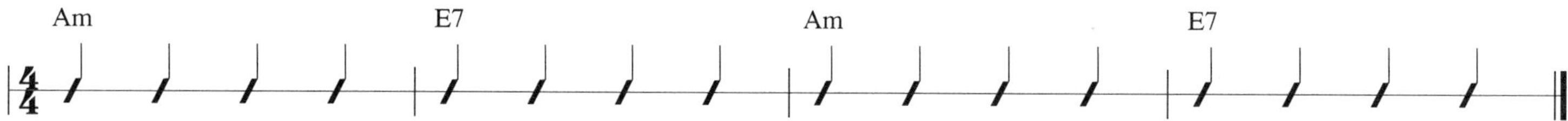

A HARMONIC MINOR - SLIDING
A-B-C-D-E-F-G♯

Because the previous harmonic minor scale is a bit tricky and awkward to finger, we thought it might be nice to have something that falls under the fingers a little easier. Plus, moving across the fingerboard in a more diagonal fashion covers more ground. Notice the symmetry of this scale—two strings with exactly the same shape and then one note on the next string. Once we slide that note up, the pattern repeats. This makes it easy to play and easy to locate. Focus on those root "A" notes. Remember that, to use a scale like this in a different key, simply start the pattern on a different note. If you need an F♯ harmonic minor scale, find an F♯ starting note and plot out the pattern. For extra credit, see if you can name the notes of the F♯ harmonic minor. (Answer at bottom of page.)

Visualize It:

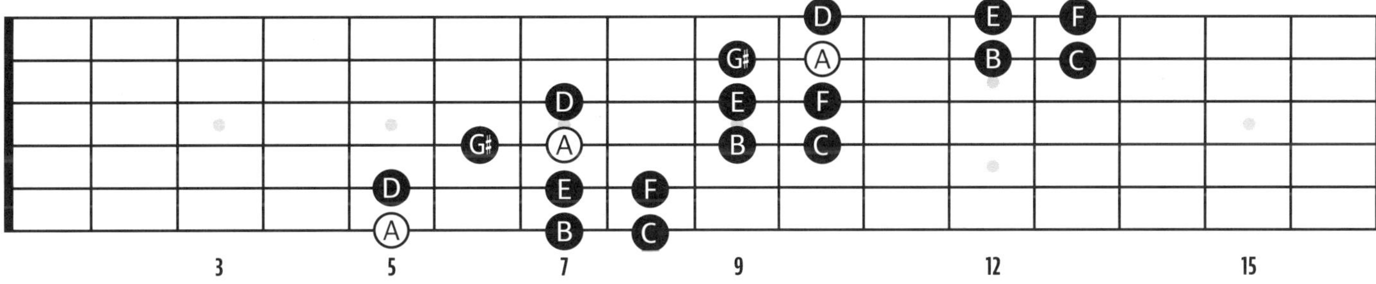

Play It:

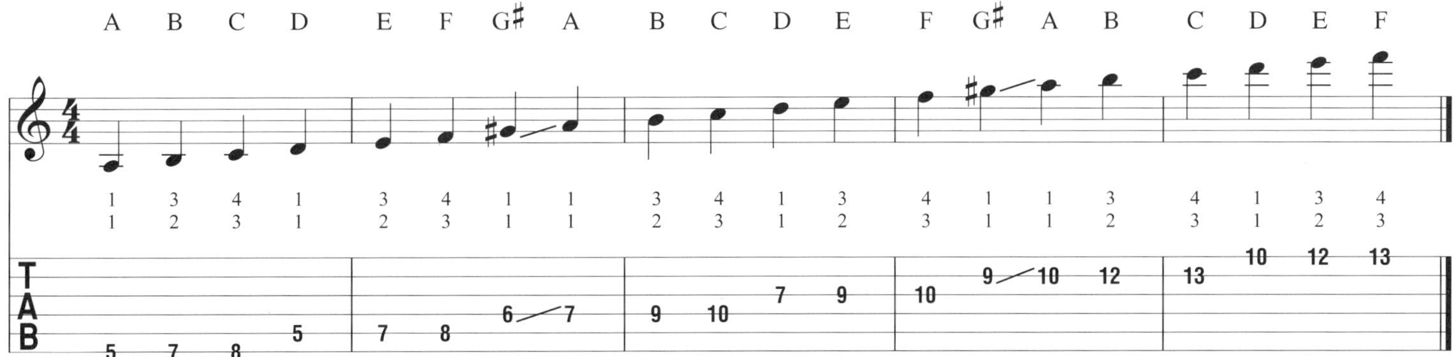

Practice It:

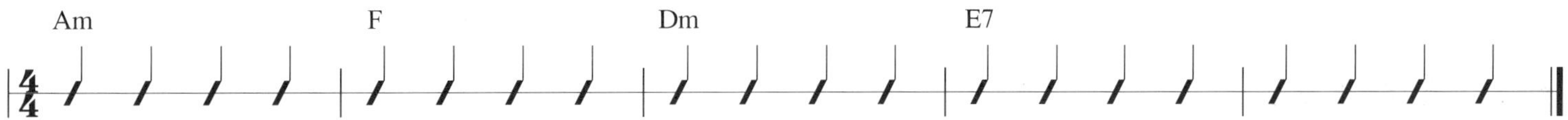

(Answer - F♯-G♯-A-B-C♯-D-E♯)

MOVABLE MAJOR SCALES

B♭ MAJOR (G SHAPE)

B♭-C-D-E♭-F-G-A

Because major scales are so important, we don't want to only know them in the open position. So now, let's learn about "movable scales." We've mentioned this briefly before when we talked about taking a scale shape and starting on a different note. We refer to that as "movable" since it's not tied down to open-string notes. Indeed, we can do the same with chords. Movable chords are also referred to as "barre chords," where we account for any open notes by barring across the frets. This allows us to take that same chord shape and generate a new chord (with the same quality) by just moving it around the neck. We'll start off here with what we'll call the "G shape," as it refers to the open G major scale we previously learned. Go back and look at that scale, then study the new fretboard diagram for this one: B♭ major. Can you see how we just took that same shape (with the open notes) and moved it up three frets? Also, visualize that open G chord within the scale. To summarize, we can take this shape and start anywhere on the guitar to get different major scales, all of which are named by the root on the sixth string.

Visualize It:

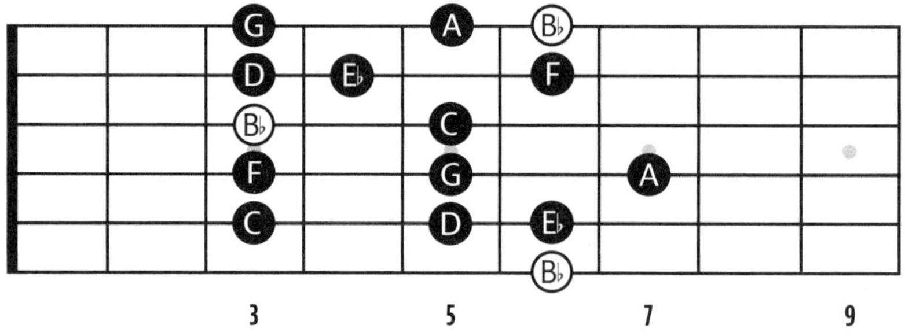

Play It:

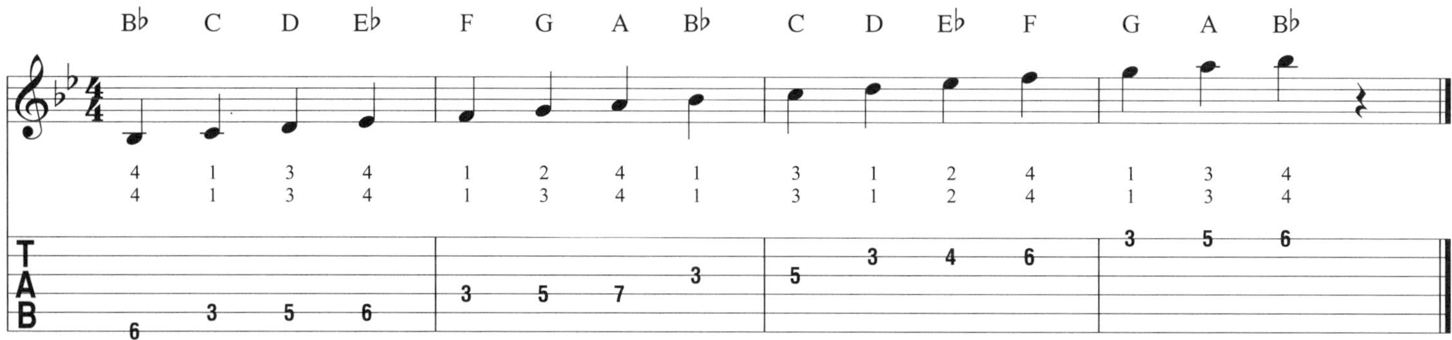

Practice It:

E♭ MAJOR (C SHAPE)
E♭-F-G-A♭-B♭-C-D

Picture that C major scale we learned in the open position. Once you recall it, let's move it up the neck three frets. Now, we have an E♭ major scale. Do you see how powerful this is? With guitar, we can learn one scale shape and use it all over the neck to get any other key. However, it's a blessing and a curse. While it makes knowing a lot of scales very simple, it's easy to overlook what notes you're playing and just play the shape. While many accomplished players get by without knowing too much theory or all the note names, I always recommend learning enough to help gain command of the fretboard. Again, try and picture that C chord embedded in the scale and use that visual to help plot the scale notes.

Visualize It:

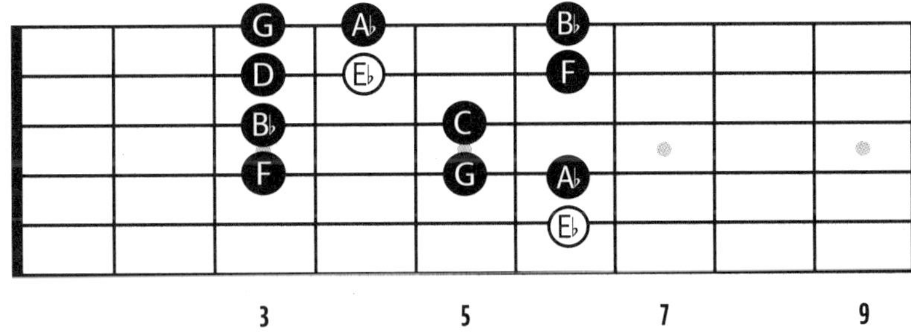

Play It:

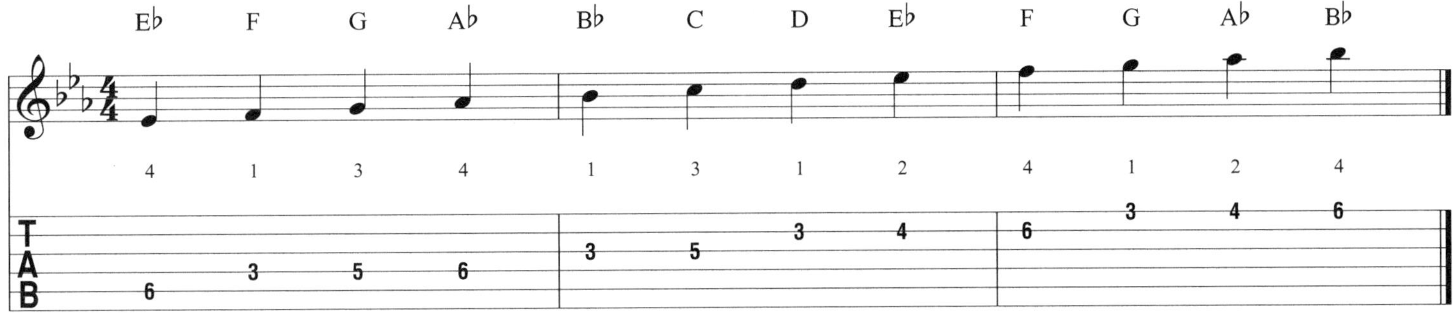

Practice It:

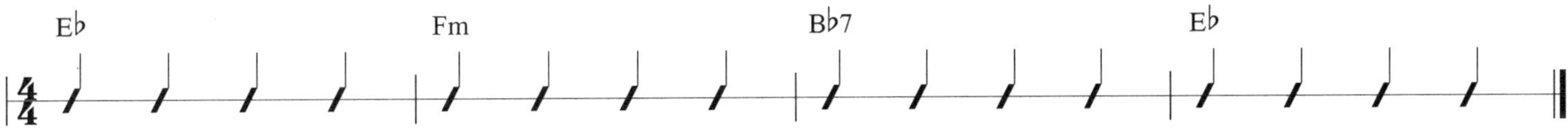

B MAJOR (A SHAPE)
B-C♯-D♯-E-F♯-G♯-A♯

The movable shapes we're learning now are part of what is called the CAGED system. CAGED is an acronym for C, A, G, E, and D chord shapes. Again, we're just taking scales that we previously learned and moving them up the neck. This concept is so important to understand on the instrument, as it will help you connect all the shapes and scales together. Eventually, this will lead to a complete understanding of the entire guitar neck. Even though this scale is only presented in one key, experiment by playing it all over the neck in different keys. Additionally, challenge yourself to recite all the notes of the scale as you move to a new key.

Visualize It:

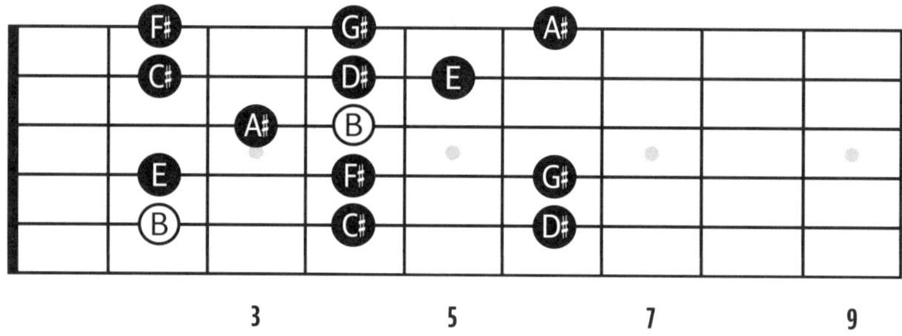

Play It:

Practice It:

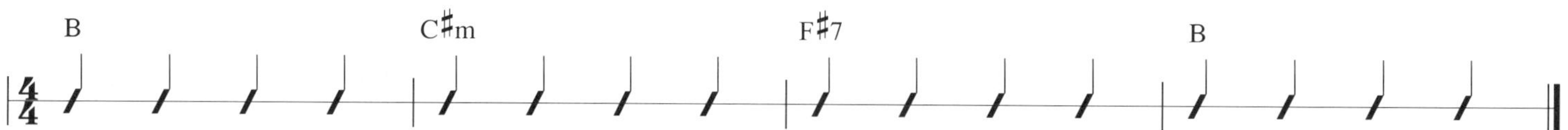

A♭ MAJOR (E SHAPE)
A♭-B♭-C-D♭-E♭-F-G

In addition to playing the scale, try and play the accompanying chord as well. (In this case, it's an E shape played as an A♭ barre chord on the fourth fret.) Then, after playing the chord, play through the scale, all the while visualizing that chord shape and how the notes connect. After all, in our improvising, we don't want to be stuck having to only play linear lines that follow the scale notes in order. Good melodies and improvisations jump around the scale. If you haven't checked it out yet, take a look at the Appendix at the end of the book. There, we show some scale sequences that you can use when practicing to get a handle on mixing up melodic lines.

Visualize It:

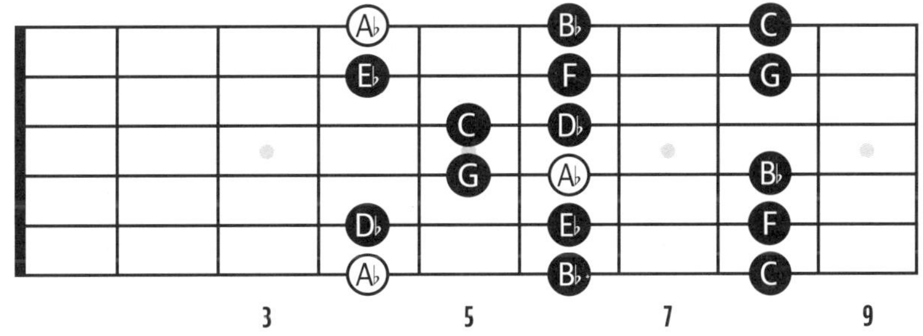

Play It:

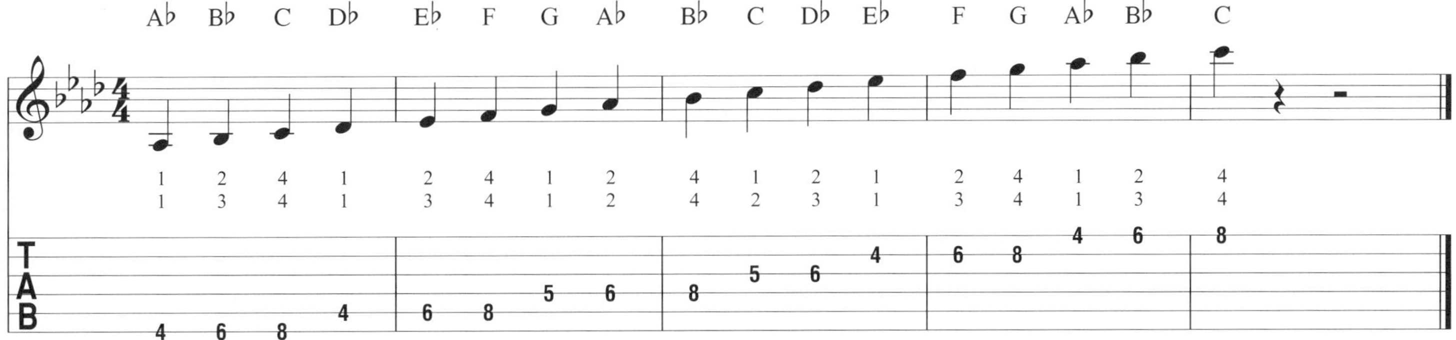

Practice It:

F MAJOR (D SHAPE)
F-G-A-B♭-C-D-E

The final shape we'll look at in our CAGED system is the D shape, which we'll play as an F major scale. Again, look for that D chord within the scale shape. As a great exercise to fully understand the power of the CAGED system, try playing one scale in all the different shapes. For example, if you want to play D major all over the neck, start off by playing the C shape, then the A shape, G shape, E shape, and finally, the D shape. Play each chord followed by the accompanying scale. Some of the chords will feel a little uncomfortable (the G shape especially). When you can do this quickly and comfortably, you will be well on your way to having a complete understanding of the notes, scales, and chords on the entire fretboard!

Visualize It:

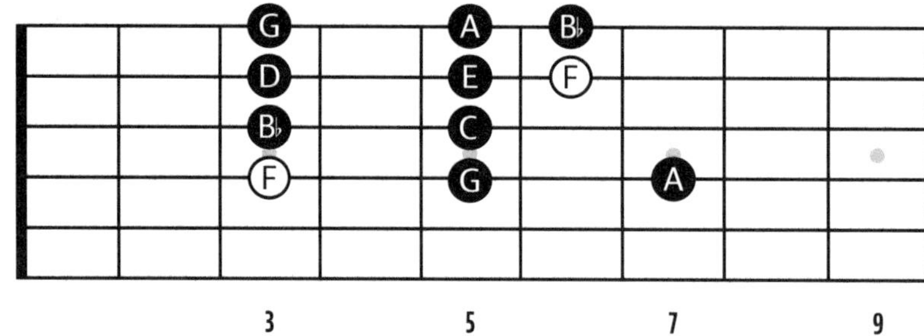

Play It:

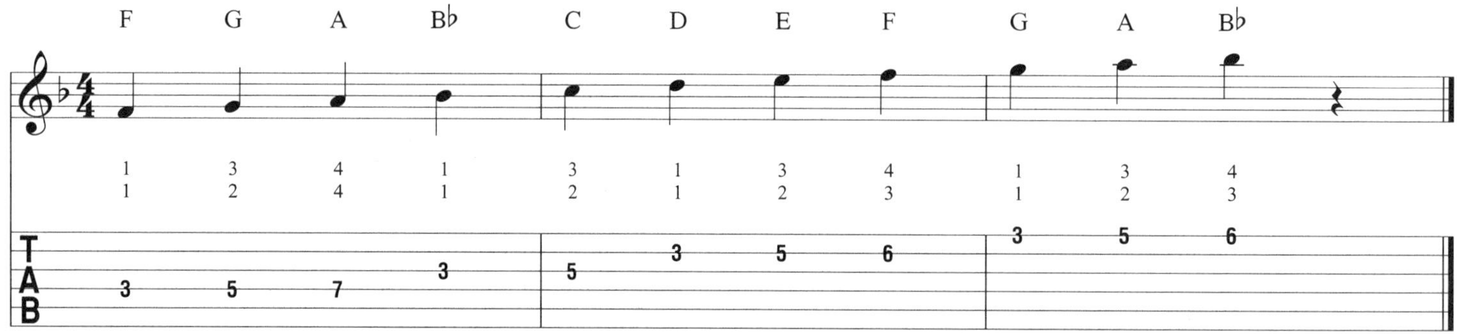

Practice It:

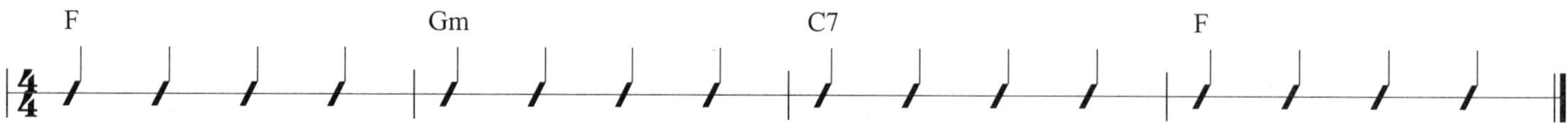

G MAJOR - THREE-NOTES-PER-STRING

G-A-B-C-D-E-F♯

Three-notes-per-string scale shapes are very popular on guitar, as they lay out in a symmetrical pattern. They also lend themselves to playing fast, as the picking pattern for the string crossings is consistent. For our G major, it's a bit of a variation on the E shape that we previously learned. Therefore, tying this to a G major barre chord at the third fret (E major shape) can be helpful. The five-fret span on the sixth and fifth strings can be a bit daunting at first, but it's well worth the effort, as the hand will get used to the stretch the more you do it. Play around with the different fingerings to see what feels more comfortable.

Visualize It:

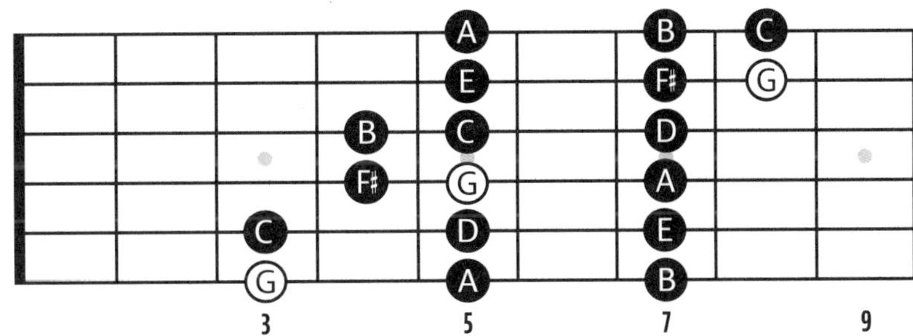

Play It:

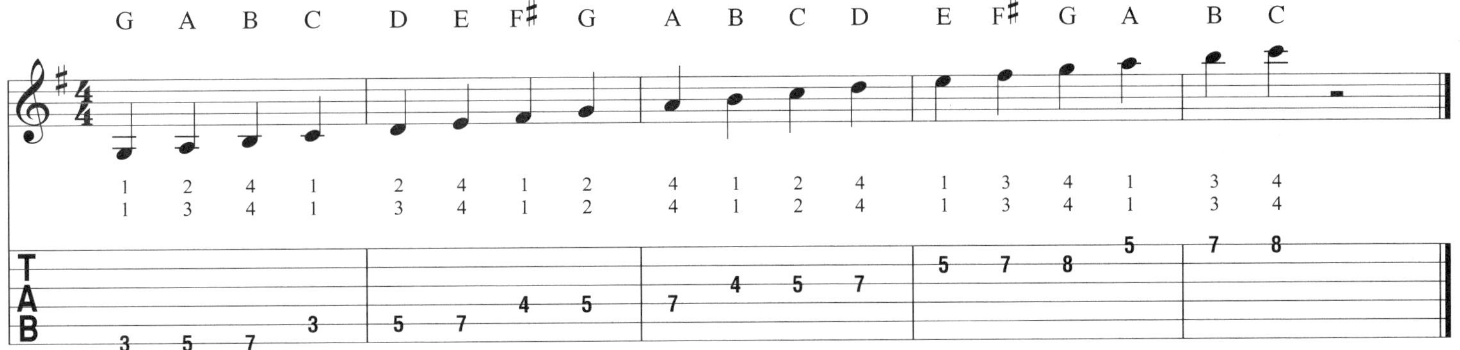

Practice It:

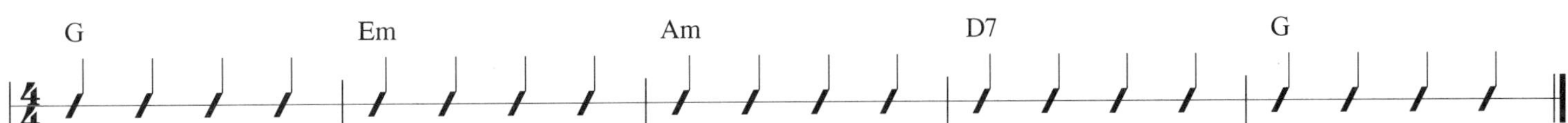

A MAJOR - SLIDING DIAGONAL
A-B-C#-D-E-F#-G#

Like the previous G major scale, we can tie this sliding scale to the E major shape—in this case, an A major barre chord on the fifth fret. This is a perfectly symmetrical shape with each pair of strings being exactly the same. Hopefully you've got your wide five-fret stretch down, since this scale uses it on all strings! This one might also help unlock some mysteries on the guitar. Notice how we're basically just repeating the same shape by moving two strings up (in pitch) and two (or three, when on the second string) frets over. It's just a system of connecting the octave notes with identical scale patterns. It's a very powerful tool to have—knowing that given any note on the guitar, you can play that shape, then repeat it on the next pair of strings.

Visualize It:

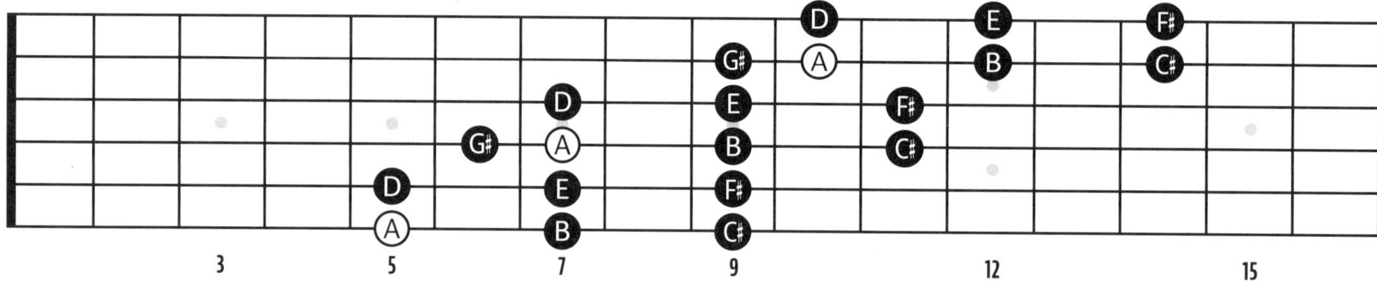

Play It:

Practice It:

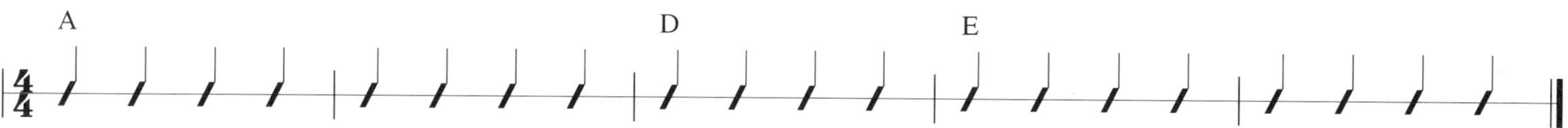

C MAJOR - THREE-NOTES-PER-STRING, FIFTH-STRING ROOT

C-D-E-F-G-A-B

We can also have a three-notes-per-string scale shape that starts with a root on the fifth string. In this case, it's very similar to our A shape pattern. Picture a C major barre chord on the third fret to help anchor the scale. It's not as symmetrical as the other three-notes-per-string shapes, but it still falls under the fingers nicely. Also, there will be instances where you'll want to have a scale with a fifth-string root as opposed to a sixth-string root. As with all these movable shapes, take some time learning them all over the neck in different keys, always keeping in mind the name of the notes while you are playing.

Visualize It:

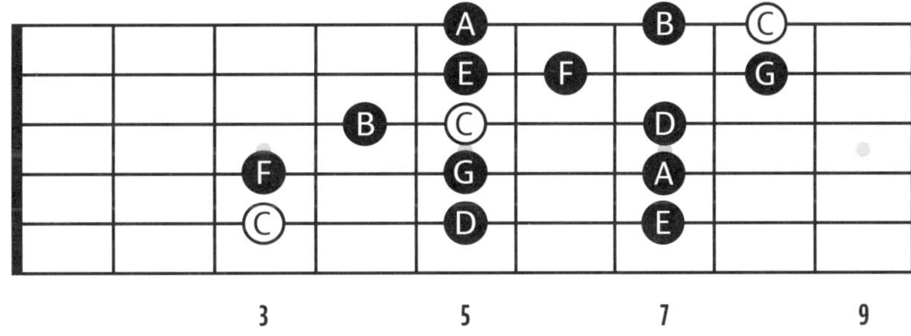

Play It:

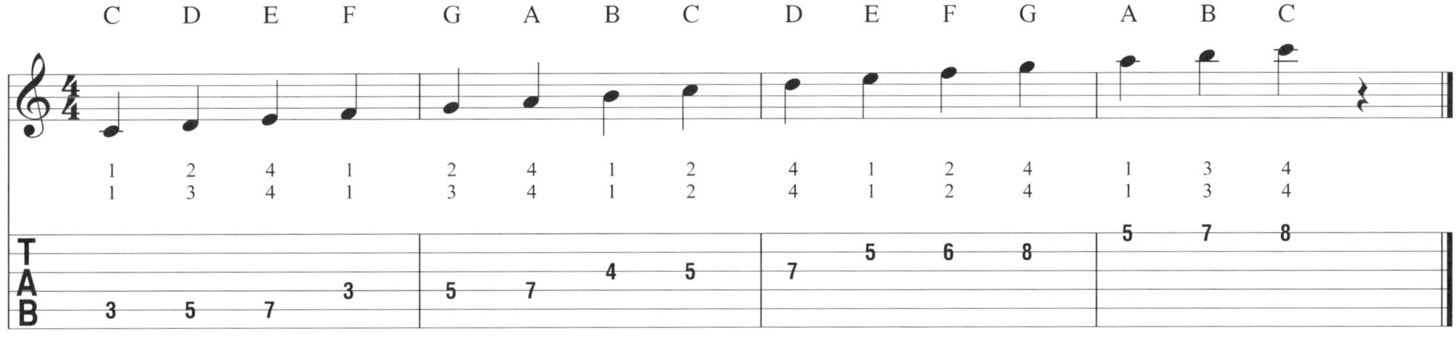

Practice It:

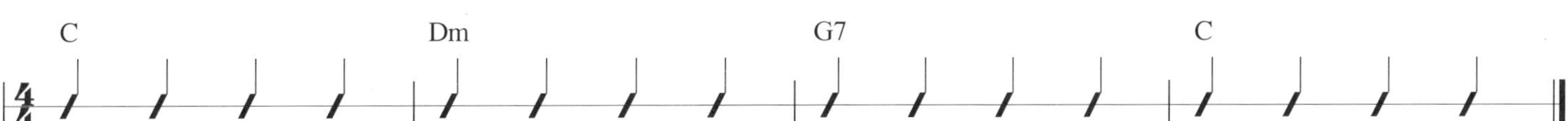

G MAJOR - THREE-NOTES-PER-STRING, FOURTH-STRING ROOT

G-A-B-C-D-E-F♯

For our final three-notes-per-string major-scale shape, we'll look at a G major scale rooted on the fifth fret of the fourth string. Once you have it under your fingers, you'll be able to play three-notes-per-string major-scale shapes rooted on any of the lowest three strings. If you like these shapes, or any that you've learned thus far, I'd also encourage you to turn them into minor scales as well. You know the formulas and (hopefully) are starting to know the notes. Taking what you know and adding to it is one of the quickest and easiest ways to gain knowledge on the instrument.

Visualize It:

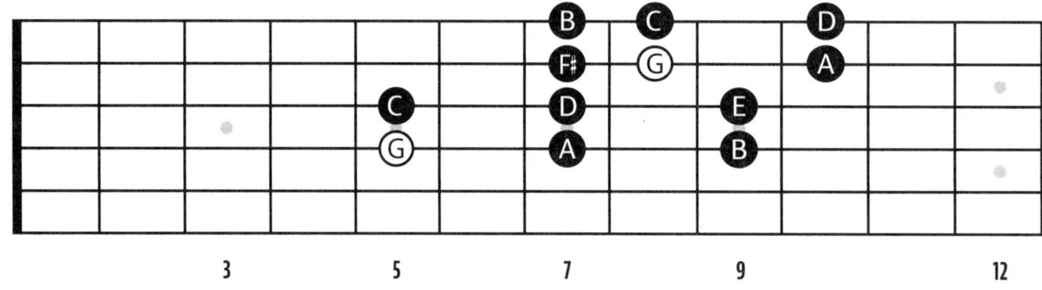

Play It:

Practice It:

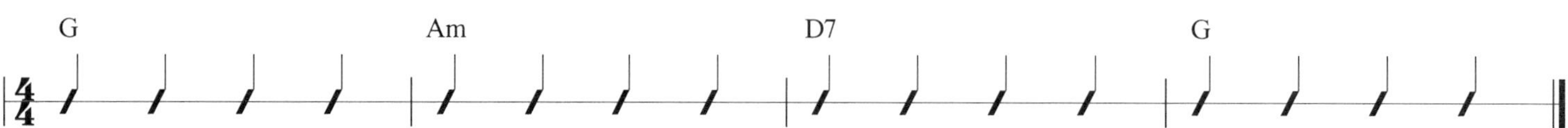

F MAJOR (ONE STRING)
F-G-A-B♭-C-D-E

One of the difficulties of learning on the guitar is the fact that the strings create different patterns of notes, making it hard at first to understand the concept of half steps and whole steps. It's super easy on a piano, as the keys are all laid out lowest to highest, left to right. All the natural notes are white keys, and the sharps and flats are black keys. So, what if we approach the guitar like a piano? Instead of playing vertically across the strings, what if we just played up and down along one string? Now it becomes very easy to see our whole steps (two frets) and half steps (one fret). This may not be the most practical way to play a scale, but it certainly is the easiest to learn. It also makes for an excellent exercise for learning the note names. Our scale here is presented in F major, but experiment with starting on any note, on any string, and find all your major scales, reciting the note names as you play.

Visualize It:

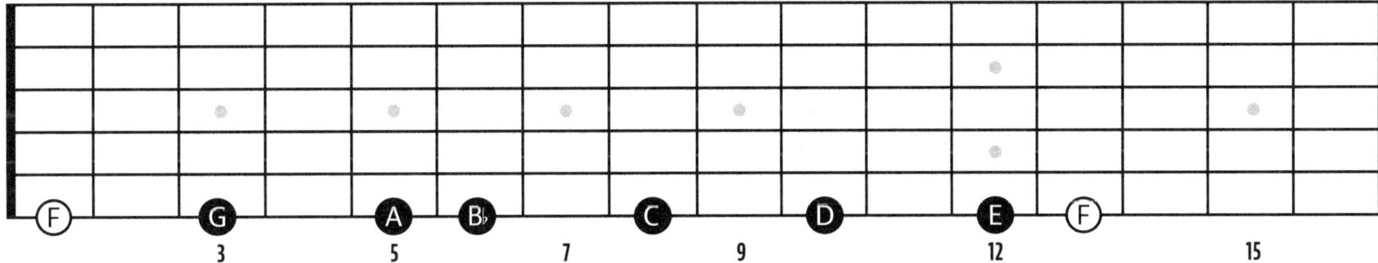

Play It:

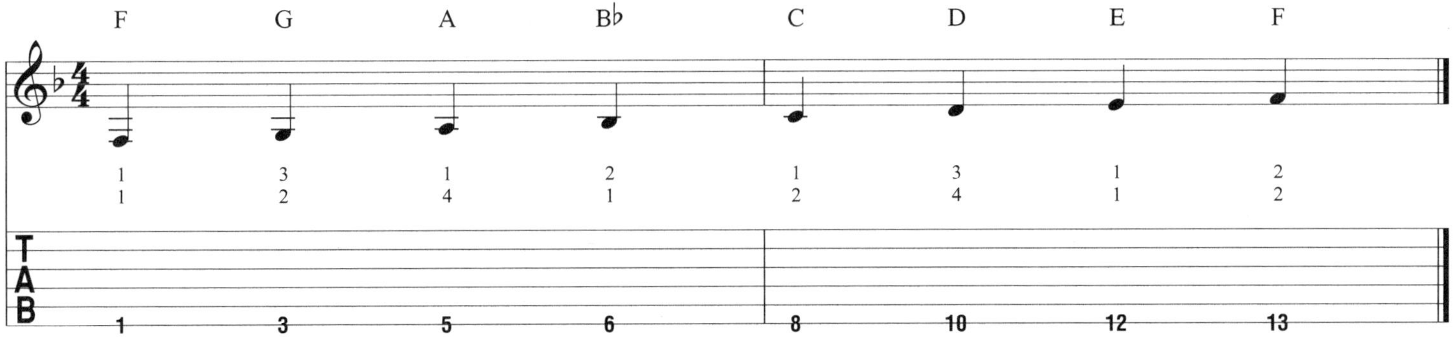

Practice It:

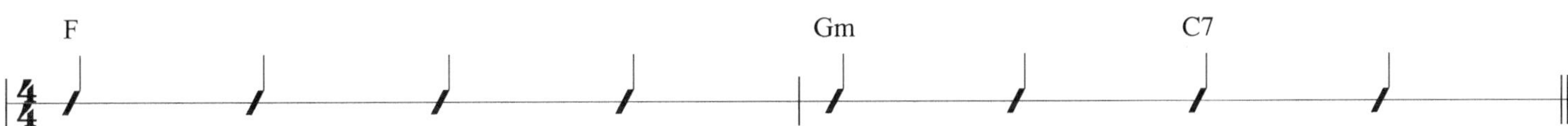

THE MODES

A DORIAN

A-B-C-D-E-F♯-G

Now we come to one of the more confusing and misunderstood topics in scale study: modes. There are really two ways to look at a modal scale: 1. How it relates to the major scale, and 2. As a stand-alone scale. In simple terms, a mode is just a scale that starts on a different note of the major scale. Therefore, we have seven modes, each starting on a different major scale tone. In fact, we've already learned one mode: Ionian. That's the major scale starting on its root note. The Dorian mode is a scale that starts on the second note of a major scale, in this case A, which is the second note of a G major scale. You might ask, "What's the big deal? We already know the major scale." Well, it's actually more about the flavor that the different modes create and looking at the chords you play each mode over. In the case of Dorian, we'll use that over a minor chord of the same root. So, we'll play A Dorian over an A minor chord. When we compare that to the scale we'd typically use (A natural minor), we see a one-note difference: the F♯ versus the F natural. That F♯, or raised 6th tone, is what gives Dorian its signature flavor.

Visualize It:

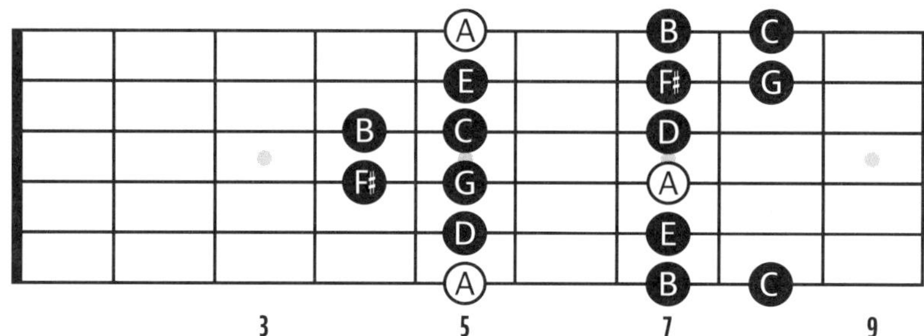

Play It:

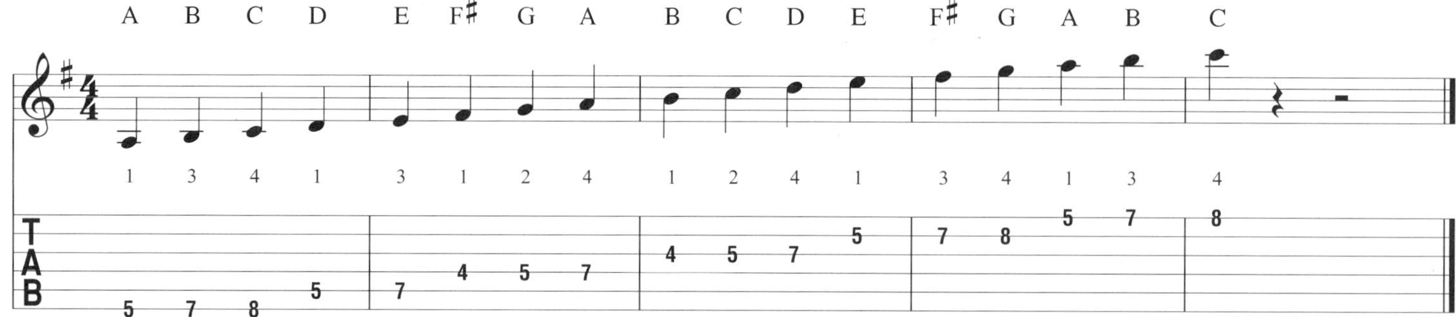

Practice It:

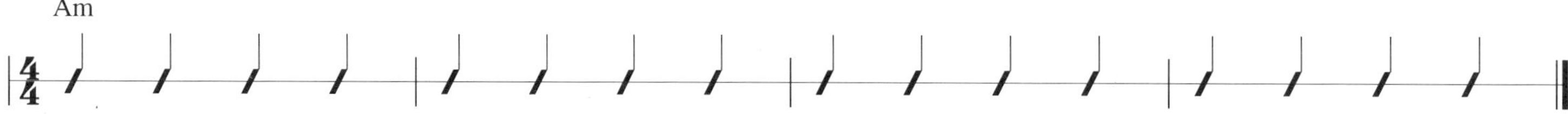

A PHRYGIAN
A-B♭-C-D-E-F-G

The Phrygian, or third mode of the major scale, is a popular scale used in Spanish music as well as metal. The A Phrygian mode contains the same notes as an F major scale but starts on an A. If you compare it to an A minor scale, it has a flatted second, B♭, as opposed to a B. That one note makes all the difference and helps create that beautiful tension. If you're confused as to why we'd call it something different, when it's really just an F major scale, it all comes down to what chords we play it over. Obviously, if we're in the key of F major, then an F major scale will sound great. But what if we have an extended jam on a minor chord? We could use the minor scale that matches. However, if we want a little more flavor, we can spice it up a bit with the Phrygian mode. I remember learning all these modes when I was young but did not understand how to use them. When I discovered that it's all about the chords you're playing over, it made so much more sense and sounded much better! So, once you get A Phrygian down, play it over our backing track. Then, swap it out with A minor and A Dorian over that same backing track to taste the different flavors of each scale.

Visualize It:

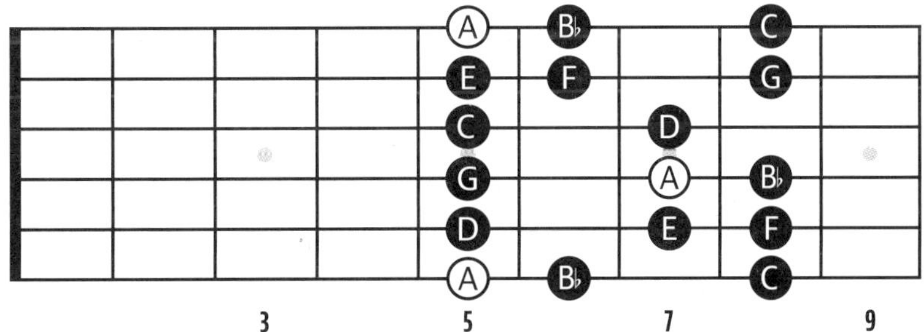

Play It:

Practice It:

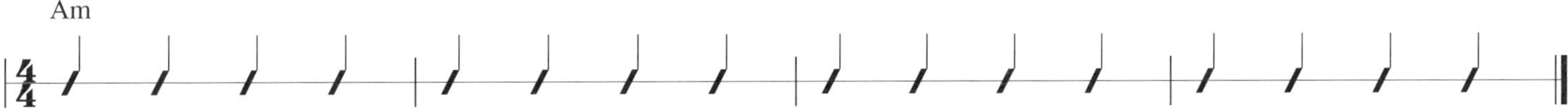

A LYDIAN
A-B-C♯-D♯-E-F♯-G♯

The fourth mode, Lydian, starts on the fourth note of the major scale. Can you recognize what major scale A Lydian is from? Take a look at those sharps. Four sharps would be the key of E major. In general, the modes we previously learned—Dorian and Phrygian—are used over minor chords. The Lydian mode, though, is most often used over a major chord. Let's compare it to A major. A major will have three sharps—F♯, C♯, G♯—while A Lydian adds the raised 4th, D♯. This gives a very ethereal or cosmic "floating through space" type of sound. For a great example of the Lydian mode, check out Joe Satriani's "Flying in a Blue Dream." After looking at several modes now and analyzing them, you might be asking the question, "Can't I just play the major scale that the mode comes from?" And the answer is "yes, absolutely." After all, they are the same notes, and it's not like you want to always start your improvising or melodies on the start of the scale. As long as you understand the concept of where to use the mode, notes are notes, and there's no difference except for the analysis in music theory. In other words, to effectively play A Lydian all over the neck, feel free to view it as E major and use any shape or pattern that you are comfortable and familiar with.

Visualize It:

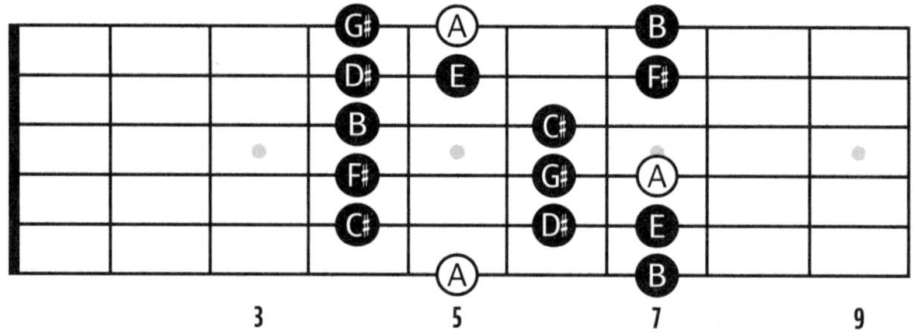

Play It:

Practice It:

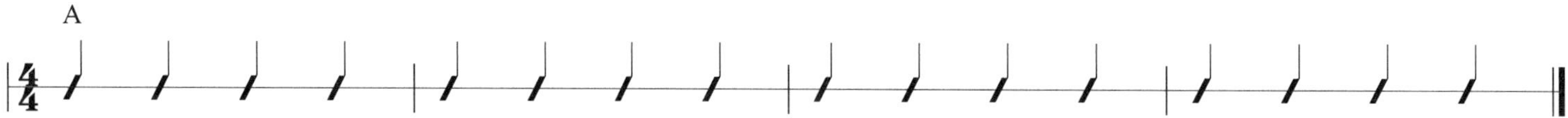

A MIXOLYDIAN
A-B-C♯-D-E-F♯-G

Mixolydian is the fifth mode of the major scale and starts on the fifth note of that major scale. In order to determine what major scale A Mixolydian is from, we have to ask, "what major scale contains A as the 5th?" So, this is where knowing your major scale notes and formulas becomes very useful. A is the 5th of D, so A Mixolydian has the same notes as D major. Major scales are the building blocks of all other scales, which is why we have so much focus on learning major scales early in the book. If you're having a difficult time understanding where we're at, go back and brush up on those major scale details. When you're ready, check out how the A Mixolydian sounds played over the dominant seventh chord heard in our backing track. Mixolydian is often a go-to scale for a dominant seventh chord of the same name. (D7 = D Mixolydian, A7 = A Mixolydian, etc.)

Visualize It:

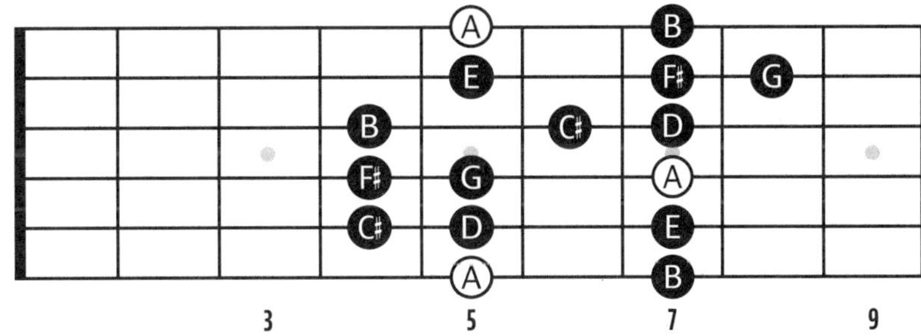

Play It:

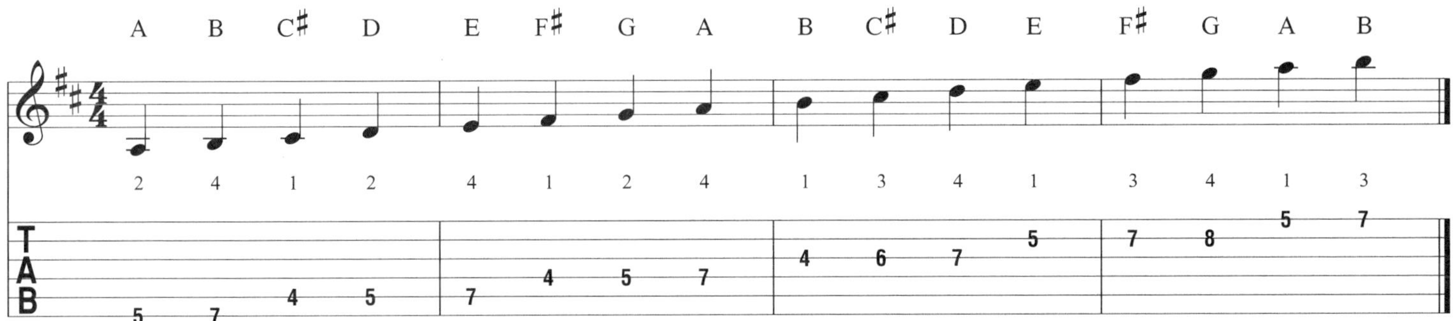

Practice It:

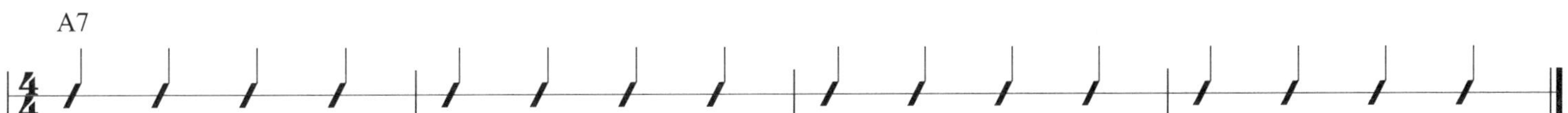

A AEOLIAN
A-B-C-D-E-F-G

The Aeolian mode, or natural minor scale, is the 6th degree of the major scale. Do you remember when we talked about relative major and minor? Our natural minor scale can also be labeled as Aeolian. In the case of A Aeolian, A is the 6th degree of C, so here we find the same notes as C major. Remember of course, C major and A minor have that relative major/minor relationship. In fact, it would be a great idea to become familiar with the relative minor scale (Aeolian scale) for every major scale. Although we already learned a version of the A minor scale, the Aeolian mode is so often used that it bears repeating. Furthermore, since these scales are movable, you now have access to all 12 minor keys. Let's also take a look at how this mode relates to the minor pentatonic. Can you see the A minor pentatonic shape within the Aeolian mode? The Aeolian mode adds two notes: B and F. When playing with the backing track, switch between the minor pentatonic and the Aeolian mode to get a feel for the flavor of those added notes.

Visualize It:

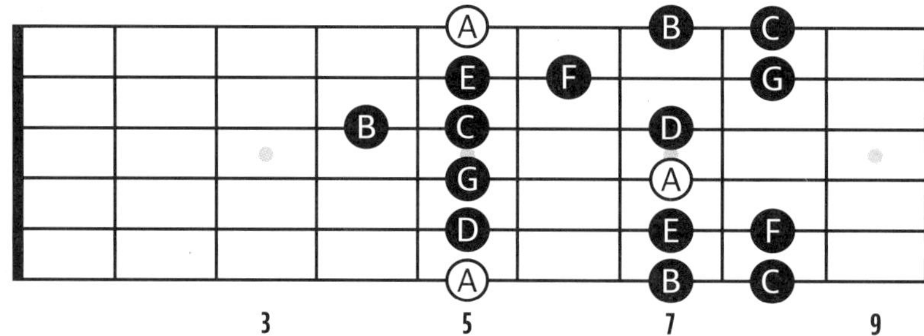

Play It:

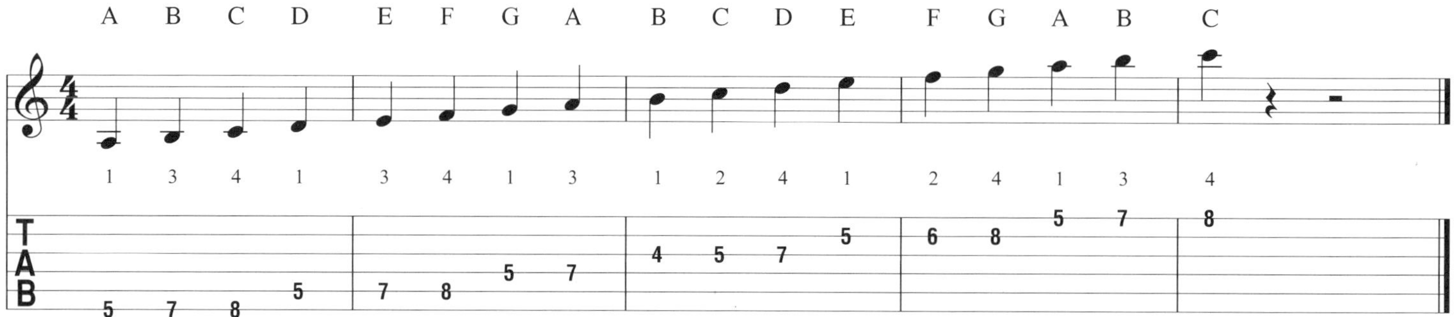

Practice It:

A LOCRIAN
A-B♭-C-D-E♭-F-G

The seventh and final mode of the major scale is Locrian, based on the seventh note of a major scale. For A Locrian, we'll be looking at the notes of B♭ major, since A is the seventh note of the B♭ major scale. The Locrian mode is often described as having a lot of tension. The notes form a dark-sounding m7♭5 chord that generally wants to resolve. This one might take a bit of getting used to for your ear to accept. If you're looking for some extra credit, here's a great way to try out the modes, all while learning the fingerboard. Take an open string—let's first use the sixth string—and play all the different "E" modes, occasionally hitting the open E and letting it ring. For example, try E Ionian, E Dorian, E Phrygian, E Lydian, E Mixolydian, E Aeolian, and E Locrian. This will give you a sort of backing track to help you hear what the modes sound like over their home or root. You can use any shape that you like. Remember, the modes are just major scales that start on different notes. E Dorian = D major, E Phrygian = C major, E Lydian = B major, E Mixolydian = A major, E Aeolian = G major, and E Locrian = F major. So, do some deep thinking, find those modes, and train your ear. This exercise will also work well with the open fifth string, using all the "A" modes, as well as the open fourth string, using all the "D" modes.

Visualize It:

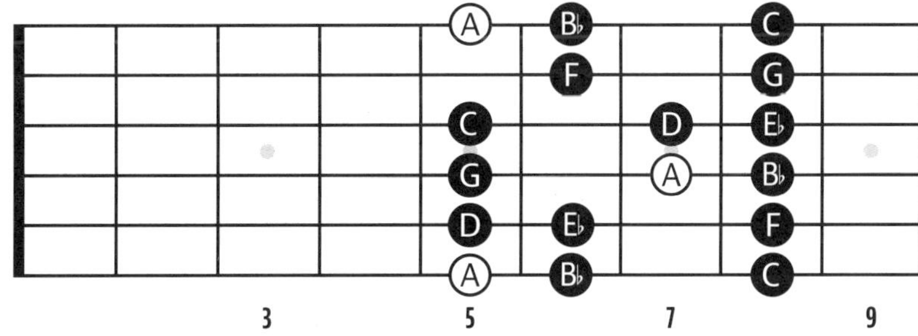

Play It:

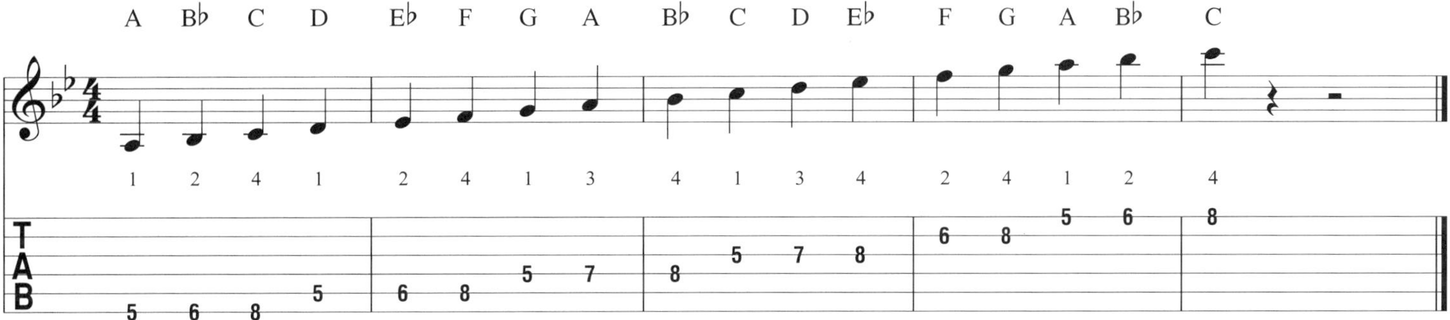

Practice It:

OUTSIDE SCALES

A LYDIAN DOMINANT

A-B-C♯-D♯-E-F♯-G

The Lydian dominant scale is the fourth mode of the melodic minor scale. Yes, major scales aren't the only scales that have modes! While the focus of this book was to get the most used and practical scales under your fingers, we'd be remiss if we didn't include some "outside scales." These scales are generally used in jazz over dominant seventh chords. They are considered "outside," as they have notes that don't fall into the diatonic harmony of a given key. Mainly used to create tension when improvising, the Lydian dominant will not create a nice melody to play over a pop-rock chord progression. However, it will be a great choice when soloing over some dominant seventh chords and can also be used if you want to jazz up the blues.

Visualize It:

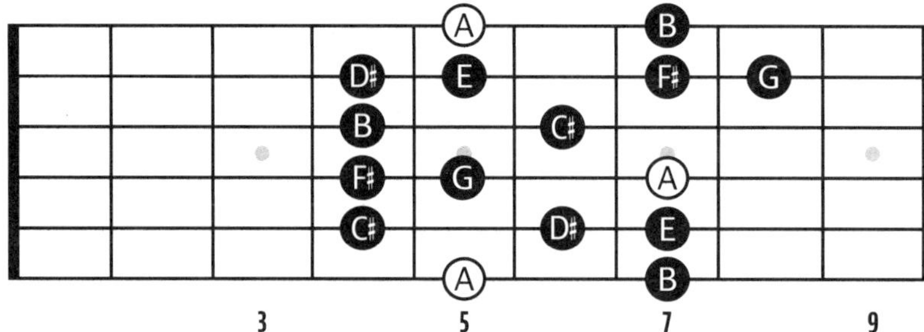

Play It:

Practice It:

A PHRYGIAN DOMINANT
A-B♭-C♯-D-E-F-G

Phrygian dominant is the fifth mode of the harmonic minor scale and is sometimes called the Spanish Phrygian or Spanish Gypsy scale. It's used in Middle Eastern music, as well as Flamenco. An example of this scale would be the popular Hebrew song "Hava Nagila." Like the Lydian dominant, it's often used in jazz improvising over a dominant seventh chord to imply some tension that typically resolves to a minor chord. For example, in the key of F, you'd have an A7 instead of the diatonic Am7 leading to Dm. Note, these outside scales are generally not something you'd play for an extended amount of time but rather are great to use for a measure or two as tension. So, don't mistakenly think you'll sound great if you try the Phrygian dominant scale next time you solo over a pop tune. If used for a moment in jazz or blues to add some extra tension, though, you'll sound brilliant!

Visualize It:

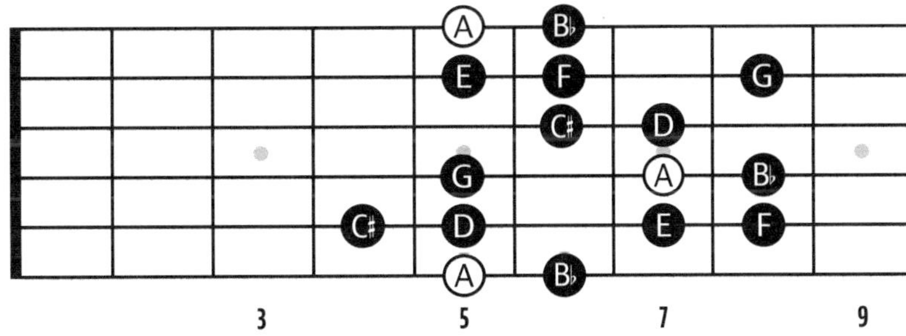

Play It:

Practice It:

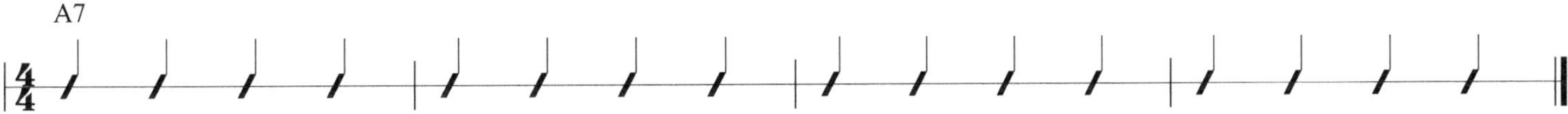

A HALF-WHOLE DIMINISHED
A-B♭-C-C♯-D♯-E-F♯-G

The half-whole diminished scale is a symmetrical scale built by alternating half steps and whole steps. If you try playing these notes all on one string, it will be easy to see the pattern. This is an eight-note scale primarily used for soloing over a dominant seventh chord. Because the scale is symmetrical, the A half-whole diminished scale also has the same notes as C half-whole diminished, D♯ half-whole diminished, and F♯ half-whole diminished. How about that for value? Four scales for the price of one! There is also a whole-half diminished scale built on alternating whole and half steps. It's generally more limited in usage and is mainly played over a diminished seventh chord.

Visualize It:

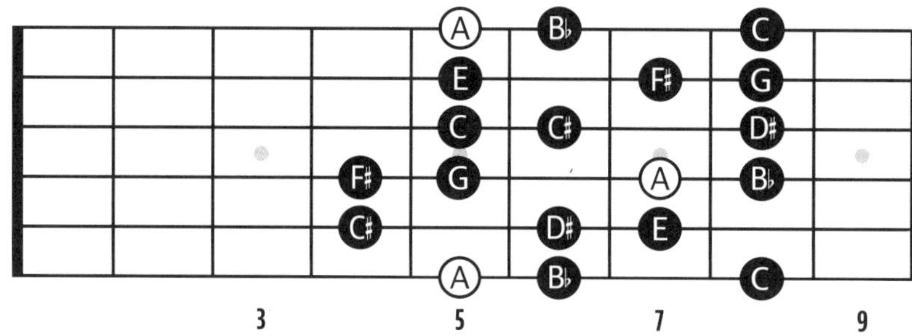

Play It:

*Due to its symmetrical nature, the diminished scale has been written out with no key signature.

Practice It:

A WHOLE TONE
A-B-C♯-D♯-F-G

The whole tone scale is simply built on all whole tones (whole steps). Again, lay this out on a single string, and it will be obvious. Every note in succession is a whole step (two frets) away from the last note. Since it's symmetrical, there are really only two whole tone scales: A and B♭. If you build a whole tone scale from any other notes, they will all be the same. Again, this scale will add some flavor and tension to a dominant seventh chord. If you'd like to hear a popular example, check out the intro to Stevie Wonder's "You Are the Sunshine of My Life."

Visualize It:

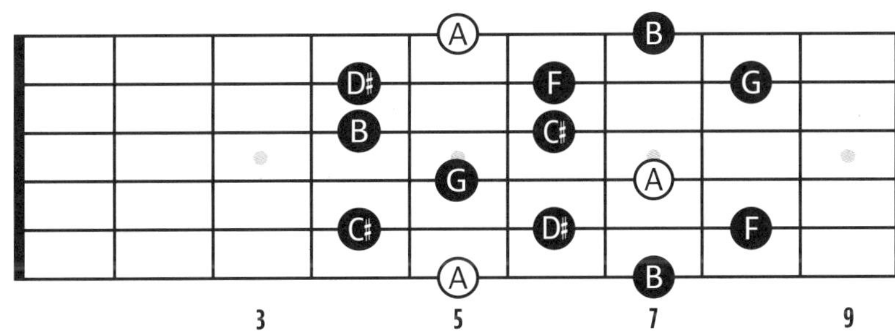

Play It:

*Due to its symmetrical nature, the whole tone scale has been written out with no key signature.

Practice It:

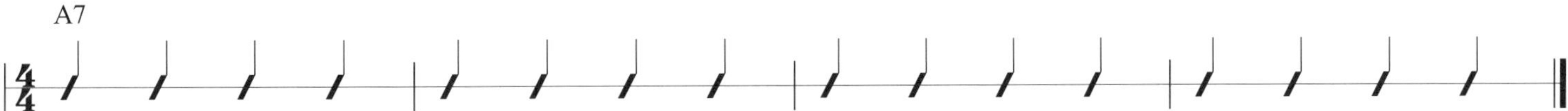

APPENDIX

Following are some practice ideas to get the most out of your scale work. We've presented these ideas using the open C major scale for a few measures recorded at a moderate tempo. Then, just continue the pattern with the rest of the scale. Once you have the idea down, try some of the other scales.

The first idea is to practice with different rhythmic variations. The second idea is to play the scale in what is called a "sequence." This will give you a more real-world experience as to how you might play notes from the scale in a musical passage or improvisation. You can even combine the two ideas and play some rhythmic variations with a scale sequence. There's an endless amount of rhythmic variations and scale sequences, so once you play through the examples and understand the concept, feel free to create some of your own. Start off slowly at first, use a metronome, and make sure you play evenly and cleanly in a relaxed manner. The tempo on the audio is only a demonstration. You can play these exercises as slowly as you need. The main takeaway from the exercises is that there are countless patterns and fingerings available to you when playing scales.

RHYTHMIC VARIATIONS

SCALE SEQUENCES

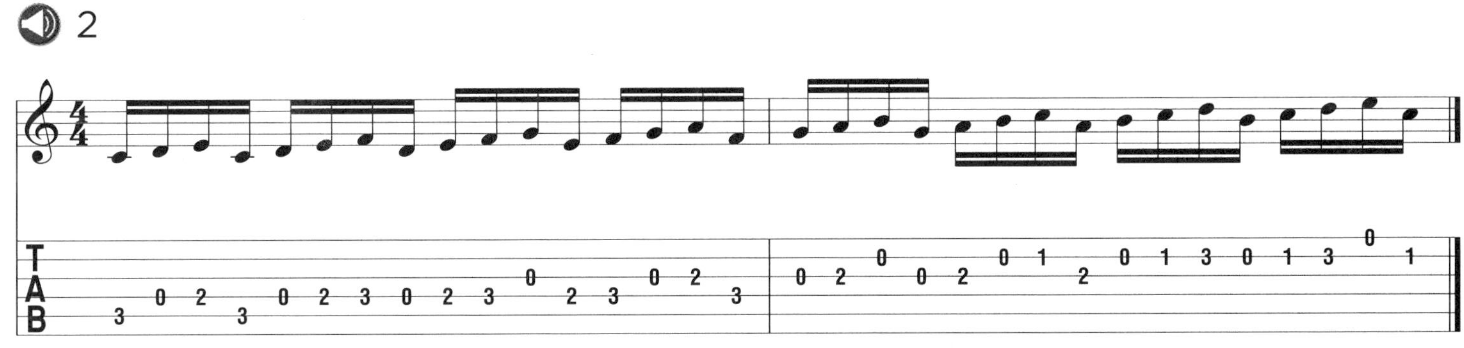

3

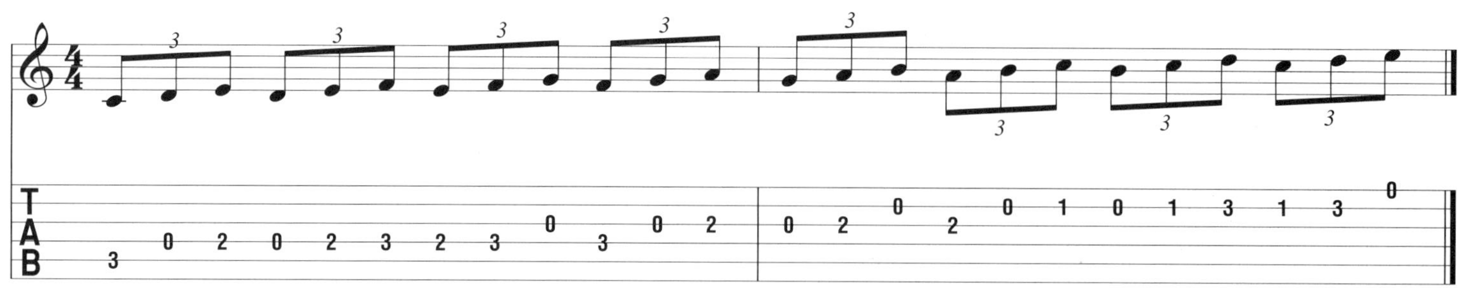

4

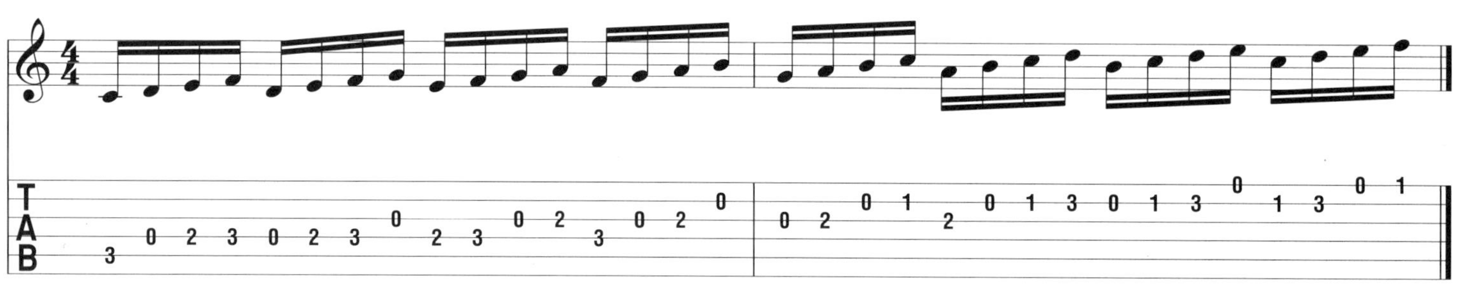

5